HENRY VII

By the same author

The Real Francis Bacon
I was James the Second's Queen
King James the Third of England
Nell Gwyn
The Great Seamen of Elizabeth I
Charles the Second's French Mistress
James Duke of Monmouth
Marlborough the Man
Royal Westminster Abbey
Charles the Second's Minette
The Duchess Hortense
King Richard II
Edward III
Robert Louis Stevenson
Henry IV
King James VI of Scotland & I of England
King William III

HENRY VII
The First Tudor King

Bryan Bevan

The Rubicon Press

The Rubicon Press
57 Cornwall Gardens
London SW7 4BE

British Library Cataloguing in Publication Data

A catalogue record for this book is available from the British Library.

ISBN 0-948695-70-6 (hbk)
ISBN 0-948695-65-X (pbk)

Printed and bound in Great Britain by Biddles of Guildford
and King's Lynn

CONTENTS

LIST OF ILLUSTRATIONS

Cover illustration: Henry VII by an unknown artist. *By courtesy of The National Portrait Gallery, London.*

Henry Tudor as a young man. Mid-sixteenth century drawing by Jacques le Boucq. *By courtesy of Mediatheque Municipale d'Arras.*

Henry VII in the transept window of Great Malvern Priory Church. *By courtesy of Felix R. Gameson.*

Queen Elizabeth of York by an unknown artist. *By courtesy of The National Portrait Gallery, London.*

Arthur, Prince of Wales (1486-1502) by an unknown artist. *By courtesy of The Royal Collection © 2000, Her Majesty Queen Elizabeth II.*

Catherine of Aragon by Michel Sittow. *By courtesy of the Kunsthistorisches Museum, Vienna.*

Henry VII's chapel in Westminster Abbey showing roof vaulting . *By courtesy of the National Monuments Record (Crown Copyright).*

Tomb effigies of Henry VII and Queen Elizabeth by Pietro Torrigiano in Westminster Abbey. *By courtesy of the National Monuments Record (Crown Copyright).*

Effigy of Henry VII by Pietro Torrigiano in Westminster Abbey. *By courtesy of the Warburg Institute, London.*

FOREWORD

BRYAN BEVAN
1913-1999

Sadly, Bryan Bevan died in March 1999 before he could witness publication of his final book. The posthumous publication of *Henry VII - The First Tudor King* is therefore a tribute to the endeavours of a devoted author who worked assiduously, even to the end, on a subject he loved.

Much of Bryan's character and writing was coloured by his upbringing. Brought up on the Welsh Border and on the family estate at Wadhurst Castle in Sussex, Bryan led a varied and creative life. His mother was the daughter of the fifth Lord Grantley. Through his mother, Bryan was a descendant of the playwright Richard Brinsley Sheridan, a connection of which he was particularly proud. He also inherited a dash of Neapolitan blood that gave him a lifelong affinity with Southern Italy.

Educated at Eton and Jesus College, Cambridge, he contemplated a career in the diplomatic service but after spending 1938 as an honorary attaché at the British Embassy in Rio de Janeiro, he thought better of it. During the Second World War, he worked for the Ministry of Information. After the war, Bryan sold his Monmouthshire estate and committed himself to writing narrative history, mostly about the Stuart, Plantagenet and Tudor monarchs.

The Rubicon Press, who have published his last seven books, pays warm homage to Bryan (whose loss as author and friend is keenly felt) by completing and publishing his last work with the encouragement and active support of his sister, Wyn Murray.

It has been said that he was a survivor from another age who clung to old-fashioned values and devoted himself to writing elegant books, the results of which are entertaining because of his shrewd judgement of human beings and an unrelenting sympathy with his subjects. Using only a lead pencil and stenographer's notebooks, and shunning all modern technology, he fashioned some wonderful books that will surely withstand the test of time.

It was a pleasure and honour to have collaborated over so many years with Bryan. He would often share wry anecdotes with us as we combed through his manuscripts over egg sandwiches and pots of Darjeeling tea, and we will always remember him with great affection for his dedication to his work, and for his shy dignity.

Anthea Page
Juanita Homan
Robin Page
(Partners of The Rubicon Press)

25th October 2000

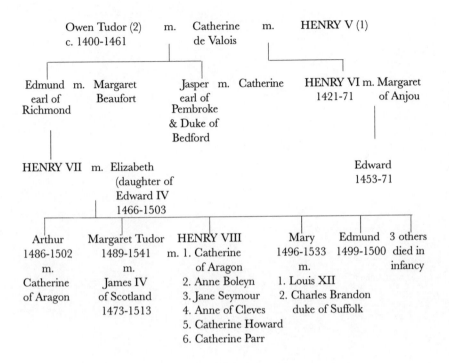

Owen Tudor (2)   m.   Catherine   m.   HENRY V (1)
c. 1400-1461   de Valois

Edmund   m.   Margaret   Jasper   m.   Catherine   HENRY VI m. Margaret
earl of   Beaufort   earl of   1421-71   of Anjou
Richmond   Pembroke
                         & Duke of
                         Bedford

HENRY VII   m.   Elizabeth   Edward
              (daughter of   1453-71
              Edward IV
              1466-1503

Arthur   Margaret Tudor   HENRY VIII   Mary   Edmund   3 others
1486-1502   1489-1541   m. 1. Catherine   1496-1533   1499-1500   died in
m.   m.   of Aragon   m.   infancy
Catherine   James IV   2. Anne Boleyn   1. Louis XII
of Aragon   of Scotland   3. Jane Seymour   2. Charles Brandon
           1473-1513   4. Anne of Cleves   duke of Suffolk
                          5. Catherine Howard
                          6. Catherine Parr

Genealogical chart showing descent and descendants of Henry VII.

I   BIRTH AND EARLY LIFE

The grandfather of Henry Tudor was a remarkable Welshman, brave, witty and high-spirited, boastful of his ancient ancestry. He was Owen (Owain) Tudor, and his family came from the Isle of Anglesey. His ancestors, particularly Ednyfed Fychan, had served the Welsh princes Llewyllyn the Great and his son David during the thirteenth century and because of them acquired substantial grants in Anglesey, Caernarvonshire and elsewhere in Wales. His descendants during the beginning of the fifteenth century were first cousins of Owen Glendower, and having earlier served Richard II, sided with Glendower against Henry IV, who had deposed Richard, in his war against the great Welsh rebel.

Owen Tudor, the son of Meredith (Maredudd) was eventually favoured by Henry V, but it is doubtful whether he served the great warrior king at Agincourt (1415). He was his page, rising to become one of the Squires of the Body. On 2 June 1420, Henry, 'too famous to live long', married Catherine de Valois, a younger daughter of Charles VI of France, who was intermittently mad, and his Bavarian Queen Isabella (Wittelsbach), a wanton princess of no morals. Catherine de Valois was nineteen at the time. After a marriage of little more than two years, Catherine was left a widow at the beginning of September 1422, for her husband had died at the Castle of Bois-de-Vincennes in France, perhaps from dysentery. It is unlikely that Henry's marriage with Catherine was a love match, for although she was within reach of Vincennes she was not even summoned to his deathbed. One son had resulted from the marriage, Prince Henry born to Catherine at Windsor on 21 December 1421, who was to succeed his father as Henry VI.

Exactly when the young widowed queen became aware of the existence of Owen Tudor we can only conjecture, but there are many stories and legends. A Welshman, Elis Graffudd, relates that Catherine first saw Owen on a summer day when he and his friends were swimming near the Court. Attracted by his handsome appearance, she arranged to meet him in disguise. Owen, however, was presumptuous enough to attempt to kiss her, almost certainly unaware of her identity. He was rebuffed. There was a struggle and the queen received a slight wound on her cheek. Later, he served her at dinner, and was ashamed of his conduct. He was soon forgiven.[1]

Catherine appointed Owen her Clerk of the Wardrobe and they soon fell in love. She was lustful by nature. At a Court dance, he is alleged to have fallen into her lap, whether by design or accident. What is very surprising is that their marriage, probably in 1425, was kept such a close secret considering the gossip and love of sensation at Court. Their children were Edmund the eldest, born about 1430 at Much Hadham Palace in Hertfordshire, a twelfth century manor owned for eight hundred years by the bishops of London, and still existing today. He was destined to be father of Henry Tudor. A year younger was Jasper, born at the bishop of Ely's manor at Hatfield. Thirdly, there was Owen, named after his father, who became a Benedictine monk at Westminster Abbey and died there in 1502, according to Polydore Vergil, the contemporary historian. One daughter, Katherine, entered a religious order, while another, Jacira, married Reynold, Lord Grey of Wilton.

Many contemporaries of Catherine's grandson Henry, subsequently Henry VII, are critical of the queen. The Italian-born Polydor Vergil, whose patron was the king, lavishly praised Owen, while criticizing Catherine. 'This woman,' he said:

> after the death of her husband ... being but young in years and thereby of less discretion to judge what was decent for her estate, married one Owen Tyder, a gentleman of Wales, adorned with wonderful gifts of body and minde, who derived his pedigree from Cadwalleder, the last King of the Britons.

Hall, the sixteenth century chronicler, tells us that Owen was comely in person 'garnished with manye godly gyftes both of nature and of grace'. He had the temerity to pay court to the young queen-mother and she, 'following her appetite, reciprocated his affections'. It all seems natural enough, but in that age a man of comparatively lowly origin would have been considered absolutely unsuitable to be the husband of a princess of France and widow of a renowned King of England.

Owen, with his deep feeling for his Welsh ancestry, was anxious that his wife should meet his relations. When they eventually met, she thought them, according to the sixteenth century writer, Sir John Wynn of Gwydir 'the goodliest doombe creatures that she ever saw because they could not speak any English'.

Eventually, about 1436, the Council of the young King Henry VI discovered the secret of the marriage. Owen and Catherine fell on evil days. Thoroughly alarmed, the Council, headed by Humphrey duke of Gloucester, Henry V's younger brother, ordered that they should be separated and deprived of their children. The two elder sons of the marriage Edmund ap Meredith ap Tydier and Jasper ap Meredith ap Tydier (as they were then called) were later committed to the care of an autocratic lady, Catherine de la Pole, sister of the earl of Suffolk, abbess of Barking, from 27 July 1437.

Earlier, the Queen Catherine had fallen seriously ill, possibly from cancer, and was now residing in Bermondsey Abbey. Henry VI, aged sixteen, only learnt of his mother's marriage to Owen Tudor in 1436 and at first can scarcely have been very pleased about it. She was to die on 3 January 1437, and her body taken to St. Katherine by the Tower, to be eventually buried in the Lady Chapel in Westminster Abbey where Henry VI later built her tomb.

According to *A Chronicle of London*, Owen Tudor was imprisoned for some time in Newgate prison, from where he managed to escape, being as resourceful as his younger son Jasper was to be in later years. It mentions in 1438:

> this same yere on Oweyn, no man of birthe, nother of lyflode (livelyhood), brak out of Newgate, ayens nyght at serchynge tyme, thorough helpe of his prest (possibly the priest, who had married him to Catherine), and wente his way hurtynge foule his kepere; but at the laste, blessyd be God, he was taken ayeyn.[2]

Recaptured and consigned again to Newgate, Humphrey of Gloucester was certainly responsible for the Welshman's imprisonment.

On reaching his majority, Henry VI granted many favours to Owen and his own half-brothers Edmund and Jasper. These included a grant of an annuity of £100 from the estates confiscated from John Lord Clinton, and the bestowal of Office of Parker of the King's Parks in parts of Denbighshire, North Wales. He also handsomely rewarded Edmund and Jasper with the earldoms of Richmond and Pembroke in 1452. Both would become fierce and loyal champions of the Lancastrian cause when the Civil War erupted between the Lancastrians and the Yorkists. It was a real tragedy that such a feeble sovereign as King Henry VI should have reigned in the 1450s, suited as he was to the life of the cloister rather than to lead armies in battle.

In his biography, Dr. Bertram Wolffe examines Henry's personal rule, his failure to maintain justice, his rewards to worthless ministers and his loss of most of the lands his father had acquired in France.[3] It may be possible to think of Henry as a royal saint, but the traditional view cannot really be sustained. He was very fond of Edmund and Jasper and it was largely owing to him that Edmund was married in 1455 to the Lady Margaret Beaufort, a girl scarcely aged twelve. Margaret, a great heiress, born at Bletsoe Castle in Bedfordshire was the only daughter of John Beaufort III, duke of Somerset and his wife Margaret Beauchamp of Bletsoe. She came of illustrious forebears, her great-grandfather being John of Gaunt, younger son of Edward III. Another renowned ancestor was her great-uncle Cardinal Henry Beaufort, a statesman of considerable ability and rival of Humphrey of Gloucester. An important character in Shakespeare's *Henry VI*, he was known for his ambition and avarice. John of Gaunt, duke of Lancaster, had married for the third time his long-time mistress Katherine Swynford, sister-in-law to the poet Chaucer, and one or two of their children were born at Beaufort Castle in France. They were made legitimate in 1397 by Richard II to please his uncle when he needed his support. His successor Henry IV, unsure of his title during his short reign, for he was an usurper, had a law passed through parliament expressly excluding them from the throne *excepta dignitate regali* (the royal dignity excepted). It has been contended that this was illegal.

It must be borne in mind that Margaret Beaufort had already been nominally married to John de la Pole, heir of the duke of Suffolk. They were both infants at the time and the marriage had been dissolved.

It is probable that Margaret grew attached to Edmund during their short marriage. His life was very brief, for he was to die aged twenty-six. He was a fighting man, who had served in Wales in 1456, but we do not know the cause of his death, probably in Carmarthen Castle on 3 November. He was firstly buried at the Greyfriars, Carmarthen, but long after his decease, his body was removed to St. David's Cathedral.

John Fisher, bishop of Rochester, an intimate friend of Lady Margaret in her later life, related when making a funeral speech for Henry on 8 September (1509), how she had hesitated before committing herself to Edmund. As a nine-year-old girl:

> I have heard her tell many a time, as she lay in prayer calling up St. Nicholas, whether sleeping or waking she could not answer, but about four o'clock in the morning one appeared unto her arrayed like a bishop and named unto her Edmund, bade take him unto her husband.

This strange vision the pious girl related to her parents.

Henry Tudor, the subject of this study, was never to know his father, for he was born posthumously three months after his father's death. His mother Margaret, not quite fourteen, gave birth in Pembroke Castle to her only son Henry on 28 January 1457. It was St. Agnes day and she was to refer to his birth many years later in a letter to her son from Calais on St. Agnes day (1501), 'the day on which I did bring into this world my good and gracious prince, king and only beloved son'. Very little notice was taken of Henry's obscure birth, for nobody could conceive that the infant earl of Richmond would become King of England twenty-eight years later. He was born in a small room in the outer ward with a fireplace. When John Leland, the antiquarian, visited Pembroke Castle in 1538, he wrote:

> In the outer ward I saw the chamber where King Henry VII was born, in knowledge whereof a chimney is new made with the arms and badges of King Henry VII.

Pembroke Castle was for some time the stronghold of Henry's uncle Jasper earl of Pembroke, who was of vital significance in his life for Henry was to owe much to Jasper. Pembroke Castle was no longer such a grim fortress, for Jasper had embellished the domestic buildings with fireplaces and a fine oriel window. Henry was very delicate in infancy, and it is probable that he owed his life to his devoted mother's loving care. As a very young mother she had also suffered in health. She was of very small stature, according to Dr. John Fisher, writing much later.

Henry was only partly Welsh, though he certainly inherited many Welsh traits of character and passed the first fourteen years of his life mainly in Pembrokeshire and Raglan Castle in Monmouthshire. As already stated, his mother was in fact English, while his paternal grandmother Catherine de Valois was French and Bavarian through her mother. Only his paternal grandfather Owen was wholly Welsh. For Henry it was wise later to make political capital out of his Welsh ancestry. For instance, he flaunted the red dragon banner of Cadwalleder, last King of the Britons.

He was born during a period of horrifying turbulence and violence, the bloody Civil War known as the 'Wars of the Roses' lasting from 1455 to the Battle of Stoke in 1487. The pathetic Henry VI was opposed by the Yorkists under Richard Plantagenet duke of York, whose claim to kingship was based on the law of primogeniture. He was directly descended from the third son of Edward III, Lionel of Clarence, through the female line, but he was killed at Wakefield (1460), to be succeeded by his eldest son Edward, a ruthless and brilliant soldier, who was to ascend the throne as Edward IV in March 1461. The wars were essentially between the great landed magnates.

Henry's mother was small and dignified, possessing a very gracious manner. Her eyes were grey and eyebrows dark and arched, her mouth rather full. She might be later grave, yet a smile sometimes lightened her face. She was an outstanding personality in her own age and indeed in any age. With a reputation for severity, there were various lighter features in her character. Pietro Torrigiano's wonderful sculptured figure of her in Mary Queen of Scot's Chapel, Westminster Abbey, is rather severe, but is considered his best work. She was a formidable and dominating character, loved by those who knew her best. Highly intelligent, she watched from afar when frequently separated from her son in early life, vigilant to take advantage of any favourable circumstance attending Henry's interests. Above all, she was keen that he should be well educated so that he might be worthy to become King of England, extremely unlikely as it might appear for many years.

E.M.G. Routh, one of her biographers wrote: 'She presents the brightest example of the strong devotional feeling and active charity of the age in which she lived ...' She is entitled to the warmest gratitude of posterity for her generous patronage of the learned and her munificent provision for the advancement of science and literature. At the universities she is chiefly remembered for the endowment of the Lady Margaret Professorship of Divinity and for the foundation of Christ's College and St. John's College, Cambridge. She had her faults, including an occasional ruthlessness and some of her critics saw her in a very different light to those who eulogized her in her own and later ages. Margaret Beaufort's apparent ability to fade into the background when political matters became too heated helped her to survive periods of great personal danger. She was to be married four times, if we include the doubtful marriage to the son of the duke of Suffolk.

Jasper Tudor, Henry's uncle, experienced both triumph and disaster in his desperate fight for the Lancastrian cause. His lasting achievement was to make it ultimately possible for his nephew to become King of England. He fought at the Battle of St. Albans in 1455, and was appointed Constable of several Welsh castles where he was very popular. His life was one of constant movement and desperate adventure, having a share in the Lancastrian triumph at Ludlow in 1459 and the capture of Denbigh Castle in early 1460.

The Battle of Mortimer's Cross, fought on St. Blaises Day, 3 February 1461 was one of the decisive battles of the Wars of the Roses, and certainly one of the bloodiest. Mortimer's Cross is a quiet hamlet between Ludlow and Leominster in Herefordshire. It was a superstitious age and early that morning of 3 February, there appeared in the sky what appeared to Edward earl of March's soldiers three suns in the mist. This is a rare phenomenon called a parhelion, or mock sun, occurring only when light is refracted through icy crystals.[4] Seeing the dismay of his soldiers, Edward, aged nineteen, hastened to reassure them that it was a good omen: 'This is a good sign, for those three suns betokeneth the Father, the Son and the Holy Ghost ...' Edward's army probably numbered about 5,000 men, including many experienced archers. The Lancastrian army, commanded by Owen Tudor, his son Jasper earl of Pembroke and the earl of Wiltshire numbered about 4,000 men. Edward's Chief Captains Sir William Herbert, Sir Walter Devereux, Lord Audley, Sir William Hastings and Lord Fitzwalter were more than a match for the Lancastrians. Owen Tudor, fighting bravely, was captured, while Jasper, possessing almost a genius for escaping, and the earl of Wiltshire fled from the field. On 25 February, Jasper Tudor wrote to Roger Paleston and John Eyton, his stewards at Denbigh, attributing 'the great dishonour and rebuke suffered by the Lancastrians to the traitorous March and Herbert with their affinityes'.

There is a curious contemporary account of the beheading of Owen Tudor in Hereford market-place where he had been brought together with other prisoners.[5]

> An he was be heddyde at the market place, and hys hedde sette a-pone the hygheyste gryce of the market crosse, and a madde woman kembyd hys here and wysche a way the blode of hys face, and she gate candellys and sette a-boote hym brennynge, moo then a C. Thys Owyne Tytre was fadyr unto the Erle of Pembroke, and hadde weddyd Quene Kateryn Kyng Harry the VIys modyr, wenying and trustyng all eway that he shulde not be hedyd tylle he saw the axe and the blocke, and wherin that he was in hys dobelet he trustyd on pardon and grace tylle the coler of hys redde vellvet dobbelet was rypped of. Then he sayde, "That hede shalle lye on the stocke that was wonte to ly on Quene Kateryn's lappe", and put hys herte and mynde holy unto God and fulle mekely toke hys dethe.

Thus died bravely the grandfather of Henry Tudor, to be buried in the church of the Grey Friars at Hereford, which no longer exists. Welsh bards wrote poems holding Owen in lasting remembrance.

For Jasper Tudor earl of Pembroke and the Lancastrians the spring of 1461 was a tragic period. When Edward of York entered London towards the end of February with a vast army, the people acclaimed him as the 'Rose of Rouen' (he had been born there). A few days later, a deputation of lords and commoners, headed by Richard Neville earl of Warwick offered him the crown at Baynard's Castle on the Thames. This he eagerly accepted and became Edward IV. He was crowned in Westminster Abbey at the end of June. The king was very handsome and tall, being over six foot three inches. Despite his main vice, his sensuality, Edward was kingly, a complete contrast to Henry VI, extremely able and a superb tactician as a soldier. When the Yorkists gained another victory fought on Palm Sunday in a blinding snowstorm at Towton in Yorkshire – the bloodiest battle ever to be fought on English soil – King Henry VI and his indomitable Queen Margaret of Anjou with Prince Edward, Margaret's son fled to Scotland.

Pembroke Castle was held by Sir John Skydmore for Jasper Tudor, but it was captured by Sir William Herbert – a Welshman and favourite of Edward IV, who had a high opinion of his ability. It was 30 September 1461 when Henry Tudor was three-and-a-half years old. With the Yorkists swarming about Pembroke Castle, Henry's fortunes underwent a profound change. Sir William Herbert, now Lord Herbert of Raglan,[6] was Jasper's most persistent enemy, for Jasper blamed him for being responsible for the execution of his father Owen after the Battle of Mortimer's Cross. Henry, a mere infant, was put into the custody of Lord Herbert, King Edward's commander in South Wales. His large family included a daughter Maud, and it was soon evident that Herbert was planning to marry Henry to Maud, probably instigated by Edward in return for an immediate payment of £1000. It was Edward's purpose to heal rival factions by arranging marriages between them, a policy adopted later by Henry in marrying Elizabeth of York.

Exactly when Henry's mother married her third husband Sir Henry Stafford, a younger son of the first Stafford duke of Buckingham is not known, but it was certainly before 1464. It resulted in the separation of mother and son.

Margaret Beaufort and Henry Stafford lived mostly in Woking, Surrey, then a village on the banks of the River Wey, in 'Woking Old Hall', a palatial mansion given them by Edward IV,[7] although the Lady Margaret was for Edward an object of suspicion. Margaret and Henry had many interests in common, including estate management and their marriage seems to have been happy.[8] When not engaged on visiting their many properties throughout the country, they would hunt regularly together, pursuing the fallow-buck deer in parts of Surrey and Hampshire. One is so accustomed in her portraits to see her constantly in prayer that it is pleasing to know that at least when she was a young woman she indulged in hunting. Her most recent biographers[9] mention their tour of West Country farms during 1467. Margaret's favourite house was at Sampford Peverell in Devon, but they visited parts of Somerset where she owned estates. Their own household consisted of nearly fifty retainers, and Henry and Margaret lived lavishly. During this tour Margaret experienced the joy of seeing her son Henry again, who was in the custody of Lord Herbert at Raglan Castle. Together with Henry Stafford she crossed by ferry over the river Severn from Bristol to Chepstow during October. Young Henry Tudor was not quite ten years old, and despite the long separation from his mother in early life was always to remain deeply attached to her. He had been deprived of the earldom of Richmond (in Yorkshire) five years earlier during August 1462. It was transferred to Richard duke of Gloucester, Edward's younger brother and then given to George of Clarence. A few months later, Margaret and Henry entertained Edward IV at 'Woking Old Hall' – the first time she had ever met him. Details of the splendid menu are given, including 700 oysters, lampreys and conger eels.

During the 1460s, Jasper Tudor endured years of desperate adventure in his attempts to restore Lancastrian fortunes. He travelled restlessly between Wales, Northumberland, Scotland, France and Brittany to muster support for King Henry VI, Margaret of Anjou and their son. During October 1462, he landed in Northumberland with Margaret of Anjou and was besieged in Bamburgh Castle, but forced to surrender it on 21 December. He visited Henry VI, who had taken refuge in Edinburgh, carrying letters from Henry VI to Louis XI of France, 'the Spider King' from Rouen in Normandy. Deep secrecy and subterfuge were needed to escape detection. It is related how Jasper was hidden by a gentleman of Mostyn in Flintshire. To escape by sea, the fugitive carried a load of peas-straw on his back like a peasant as he made his way to a ship at Picton Pool.[10] From there he sailed eventually to Brittany, landing there more by his own skill than that of the sailor, who manned the ship. To avoid capture, Jasper was wont to use as headquarters a fifteenth century house in North Wales.

Henry Tudor, at the age of five in 1462, was in the custody of Lord Herbert of Raglan, ennobled by Edward IV, and his wife, née Anne Devereux. Raglan Castle was the seat of the Lord Herbert, situated in the old Welsh district of Gwent. Amid magnificent scenery it was the administrative centre of the Herbert estates in South Wales, near the towns of Monmouth and Abergavenny. He was Edward IV's chief supporter in Wales, responsible for all the military operations against the Lancastrians, created Chief Justice of North Wales in 1461 and a year later a Knight of the Garter. A Welsh poet called him 'King Edward's master-lock' in Wales. According to Polydore Vergil, Henry when he later became king informed him that he was kept as a prisoner, but was honourably brought up by Anne, the wife of William Herbert at Raglan Castle. Although he was in custody, there was congenial company, including the young son of the fourth earl of Northumberland, and Lady Herbert herself, a highly competent, likeable woman. Nor was it by any means an altogether unpleasant and restrictive experience, for the Herberts had a large family and Henry may have formed lasting friendships at Raglan. We know that when Henry became king in 1485 he sent for Anne Herbert to come to London to meet him, so it is likely he retained affectionate memories of her, allowing her to return to Raglan with an escort.

Whilst in her custody, Anne took considerable care in seeing that he was properly educated. Bernard André, an early biographer, relates that one of his tutors was Andreas Scotus, an Oxford teacher provided by Lord Herbert, while the other tutor was Edward Haseley, later Dean Warwick according to Leland's *Itinerary*. Training in military matters was given him by Sir Hugh Johns, a man of some influence and property in Gower. Henry was later in 1485 to give Sir Hugh a present of £10 for some service he had done him in his tender years. Henry also learnt to ride well – one essential accomplishment. Except for one visit with his uncle Jasper to London in 1470, Henry of Richmond's first fourteen years were passed in Wales. He was highly intelligent even in boyhood, impressing his tutors by his application and quickness in learning.

Lord Herbert grew in favour with Edward IV to such an extent that the earl of Warwick, becoming jealous and a powerful enemy, determined to destroy him. Meanwhile, Jasper Tudor, active as ever in the cause of Lancaster, landed at Barmouth in North Wales, where his friend and Welsh ally Griffith Vaughan was ready to assist him on 24 June 1468 near Denbigh. Sir Richard Herbert (Lord Herbert's younger brother) attacked Jasper and the 2,000 men under his command. Jasper again escaped capture, remaining in hiding in Wales. That same year Lord Herbert succeeded in storming Harlech Castle, hitherto a Lancastrian stronghold. He was rewarded for its capture, being created earl of Pembroke on 8 September, a title previously held by Jasper Tudor.

Lord Herbert's days were numbered, however, since the earl of Warwick succeeded in defeating and capturing him and Sir Richard Herbert at the Battle of Edgecote (1469) near Banbury. Putting up a fierce fight against the rebels of 'Robin of Redesdale', William Herbert and his Welsh pikemen showed magnificent courage. After capture, they were taken to Northampton where they were beheaded a day after the battle. Pembroke was buried in Tintern Abbey. Henry, now aged twelve, remained in the custody of Anne, William Herbert's widow. Lord Pembroke was succeeded by his eldest son William, but he lacked his father's energy and ambition.

About 1465, Warwick turned against Edward IV, angrily upbraiding him for the political stupidity of his marriage to Elizabeth Woodville, a beautiful woman, lacking warmth, far beneath him in pride of birth and bent on aggrandizement of her many relations, for she was very arrogant. Warwick had wanted to steer King Edward's policy, through marriage with France, towards alliance with Louis XI rather than with Burgundy, and Edward had disregarded his advice. He could not stomach that he, the kingmaker, should be treated to the indignity of not even being informed of Edward's marriage. He became so resentful that he eventually decided to restore King Henry VI to his throne.

The Readeption (as it was then termed) or the Restoration of Henry of Windsor was to alter Henry of Richmond's circumstance. There are the intriguing scenes in Amboise and Angers, France, when the crafty and extremely clever Louis XI, an admirer of the kingmaker, had a hard task in persuading the imperious Margaret of Anjou to forgive the hated Warwick, particularly his calumnies against her and her son Prince Edward of Lancaster. Much against the queen's wishes it was proposed to marry her son to Anne Neville, Warwick's younger daughter in Angers Cathedral.

Edward IV was forced to flee temporarily abroad to the Court of his sister Margaret of Burgundy, wife of Charles the Bold, while Henry VI, a puppet king, was restored to the throne on 8 October 1470 by Warwick and his son-in-law George of Clarence (married to his elder daughter

Isabel). He was Edward IV's younger brother and temporarily estranged from him – 'false, fleeting, perjured Clarence', as Shakespeare calls him; treacherous as he undoubtedly was, Clarence was given Henry Tudor's earldom of Richmond.

About now, Henry Tudor had been taken, probably for better security to the home of Sir Richard Corbet at Woebley, Herefordshire, who had married a niece of Lady Herbert. With his changed fortunes, Uncle Jasper, now returned from exile, went immediately to Hereford to recover Henry, who was handed over to him. During Henry VI's brief restoration, uncle and nephew got to know each other very well. He took him to London for the first time to meet Henry VI. A story appears in André's *Vita* that Henry VI was moved to prophesy when gazing upon the tall boy that he would one day come to the throne. His actual words may have been: 'this is truly he unto whom both we and our adversaries must yield dominion'. It is derided by several modern historians, including S.B. Chrimes and Alison Weir, though it may well be true. Shakespeare alludes to it thus:

> If secret powers
> Suggest but truth to my divining thoughts,
> This pretty lad will prove my country's bliss.
> His looks are full of peaceful majesty;
> His head by nature fram'd to wear a crown,
> His hand to wield a sceptre; and himself
> Likely in time to bless a regal throne.[1]

Henry Tudor, an impressionable boy of thirteen, always spoke of Henry VI with deep reverence. If he was ever to attain the throne of England, it was naturally politic for him to do so.

Henry VI's readeption was to last barely five months. On Maundy Thursday 1471, Edward IV entered London in triumph, and had King Henry once again conveyed to the Tower. By Edward's Yorkist victory at Barnet (1471), fought in the misty light of Easter Sunday, his reign was consolidated. The earl of Warwick met his end in this battle. The decisive Battle of Tewkesbury followed on Saturday 4 May when Prince Edward of Lancaster also lost his life.

It was essential now for Henry Tudor and his uncle to flee overseas. They made for the coast accompanied by a few companions, and after many adventures were nearly captured at Chepstow. Recognized by enemies, they were taken into custody in Pembroke, but owing to their many friends in Wales, succeeded in escaping to Tenby on the Pembrokeshire coast. There Thomas White and his son John, prosperous wine merchants and mayors of Tenby, befriended them. Thomas concealed them in the cellar of his house, now Jasperby House in the High Street, and their effigies can be seen in the small chapel of St. Thomas, in St. Mary's Church. There was a dark tunnel from the house by which Henry and Jasper were able to escape by boat to France on 2 June 1471, intending to seek refuge at the Court of Louis XI, but adverse winds landed them in Brittany, then a separate duchy ruled by Duke Francis II. There is no evidence that there was treachery on the part of the Breton master of their boat, causing them to divert the route. It was fortunate for Henry and Jasper to be cast on the shores of Brittany because Louis XI four years later signed the Treaty of Picquigny with Edward IV. By it they would have been surrendered to the King of England. Whether or not Henry rewarded Thomas White later for helping them to escape is by no means clear, for he died in the early 1480s before Henry became king.

On landing at Brest, Henry and Jasper were given a cordial welcome by the duke of Brittany, and a promise to protect them for they were invaluable pawns in his negotiations with Edward IV and Louis XI. Polydore Vergil and Philippe de Commynes, the French contemporary historian, both maintain that the duke of Brittany surpassed himself in the role of gracious host for:

> he receved them willingly, and with such honor, courtesy and favor intertayned them as though they had been broothers, promysing them upon his honours that within his domynyon they should bee from thenceforth far from injury and passe as their pleasure to and fro without danger.

Commynes affirms that '*Le dit duc les traite doucement pour prisonniers*'.

Polydore Vergil's later description of Henry Tudor gives an impression of him as he grew to manhood:

> He was over average height, less than six foot and slender, although well built and strong with golden hair, which went thin in his later years. He had high cheekbones, hooded eyelids, blue eyes that sparkled, a high-bridged pointed nose and thin lips.

Lady Margaret followed the chequered fortunes of her only son with deep anxiety and corresponded with him. While her son was in Brittany, her third husband Henry Stafford died on 4 October 1471 (he had never been strong). She was to marry for the fourth time Thomas Lord Stanley, a powerful nobleman at the Court of Edward IV, one of shifting allegiances and necessarily wily and cunning. The marriage certainly took place before October 1473.

Henry Tudor was fourteen at the time when he first went to Brittany. Welsh historians suggest that, whilst there in his youth, Henry had a Breton mistress and an illegitimate son.[2] The name of the bastard son was Sir Rowland de Vielleville.[3] We do not know much about the life of Sir Rowland. He was certainly born in Brittany and later accompanied Henry VII to England with many others. He does not seem to have been much favoured, although knighted after the Battle of Blackheath (17 June 1497). Previous to this, Sir Rowland was among the esquires who participated in the tournaments celebrating the creation of Henry's second son as duke of York in 1494. He was also in attendance on King Henry at the reception of the Archduke Philip (son of the Emperor Maximilian) six years later. De Vielleville married a Welsh wife, Agnes the daughter of Sir William Griffith of Penrhyn. According to *A History of the Island of Mona*, 486 acres of land, besides lands in Pentraeth and Beaumaris were bestowed on him by his reputed father. Sir Rowland was certainly appointed Constable of Beaumaris Castle on the Isle of Anglesey, but not until July 1509 when Henry VIII had succeeded his father.

If it is true that Sir Rowland was really the illegitimate son of Henry Tudor – and there is insufficient evidence to be more positive – it is very fitting that he should return to Anglesey where the Tudors had originally sprung. He lived until 1527. Henry had the normal lusty instincts of a young man and it is likely that he had an affair with a girl from Brittany. He was an extremely discreet person and would have cloaked the affair in secrecy: Sir Rowland's granddaughter Catherine of Berain received some small favours from Queen Elizabeth I, but no evidence exists that she was a cousin of Elizabeth's.

From boyhood Henry had been deeply interested in the legends and stories concerning King Arthur, propagated by the Welsh bards, and now in exile in Brittany he was soon to discover that the duchy was rich in Celtic associations. It may be that Henry, after much pondering, decided to call his first-born legitimate son Arthur, if he were to marry. It must have been a considerable shock to him to hear of the death of Henry VI, so much an object of veneration, in the Tower on 21-22 May 1471. It is certain that Henry was violently murdered, and a circumstantial account by Warkworth (written soon after 1482) names Richard duke of Gloucester as the murderer, who was in the Tower at the time. If guilty of this brutal deed, it could only be by a secret order of his brother Edward IV. Henry Tudor and his mother the Lady Margaret were now the only surviving heirs of Lancaster.

Gradually, Jasper and Henry's sojourn in Brittany became more irksome. Duke Francis gave them political asylum, but they were not free to move about his duchy as they wished.[4] King Edward, aware that Henry was a threat to his kingship, made various attempts to persuade the duke to hand over his guests to him. He nearly succeeded in 1476. By this time, Henry Tudor had been separated from his uncle, much to their consternation. Henry was held prisoner in the great seven-storey, octagonal keep of Elven Castle, the home of Jean de Rieux, Marshal of Brittany, while Jasper was confined at Josselin. Henry was then moved to Vannes in the custody of Vincent de la Landelle, and Jasper elsewhere in Vannes in the care of Bertrand du Parc.

Eventually, Edward sent an embassy whose head was Robert Stillington, bishop of Bath and Wells, to the Duke Francis to assure him that he only had in mind Henry's marriage to one of his daughters. His purpose was to unite the Houses of York and Lancaster. For some time Francis resisted their entreaties, but at last agreed to them. Henry of Richmond set out for St. Malo, fearing that Edward IV's offer was far from genuine and that he was in grave danger. Meanwhile Jean de Quélence, Admiral of Brittany, who had the ear of the duke, remonstrated with his master, warning that it was folly to send Henry to England. He persuaded Francis to change his mind, who immediately despatched his favourite minister Pierre Landois to St. Malo to overtake Bishop Stillington's party. On his way to this port, perhaps fearing that he was being conveyed to his death, Henry feigned a fever. Much to their indignation, the party was delayed and Henry Tudor was removed to sanctuary. This was the last attempt of the Yorkist king to get hold of Henry, and Louis XI had no better fortune in getting the Tudor into his power.

Edward's death during early April 1483 was untimely because he had not yet attained his forty-first birthday. His lack of political foresight was mainly to blame for his failure to ensure the safe succession of his eldest son.[5] He was the most handsome of our medieval kings, a man of great charm, superb as a military tactician, gifted as a statesman, on the whole a successful king and very able, but he could be diabolically cruel. When no longer fighting battles – he had no love of war for its own sake – his weakness lay in his pleasure-loving nature and his huge appetite for delicious food and drink. The well-informed Italian Dominic Mancini relates 'that it was his habit, so I have learned, to take an emetic for the delight of gorging his stomach once more.'[6] As a womanizer he could never see an attractive woman without wanting to have her, but he cast them off as easily as he took them. He was unfaithful to his wife Elizabeth Woodville, though her beauty had enslaved him. Of his many mistresses Jane Shore (her real name was Elizabeth) was the one he loved best, an enchanting creature as Sir Thomas More afterwards related. By his wife he left a large family: two sons, Edward who succeeded his father as Edward V at the age of twelve, and Richard duke of York, married in his infancy to Anne Mowbray. She died early. There were five daughters, the eldest Elizabeth of York. Cecily was named after her paternal grandmother, the celebrated 'Rose of Raby'.

Queen Elizabeth Woodville's main defects were her insistence on the aggrandizement of her many relations, her haughtiness and arrogance. She was much disliked by her brothers-in-law George of Clarence – shallow, weak, and eloquent, but now dead since 1478 – and less openly by Richard duke of Gloucester. While Edward was alive, Gloucester had given his elder brother loyal and devoted service. As a reward Edward probably nominated him as Lord Protector of the realm and guardian of Edward V, but his last will and the codicil attached to it have not survived.

III   RICHARD III'S USURPATION

Richard duke of Gloucester was a ruthless and violent character, according to Sir Thomas More:[1]

> He was close and secrete, a deipe dissimuler (dissembler), lowly of countynaunce, arrogant of heart, outwardly coumpinable where he inwardly hated, not letting to kisse whome hee thoughte to kyll ... where his advantage grew, he spared no man's deathe, whose life withstood his purpose.

More accuses Richard of slaying with his own hands King Henry VI, though one would have thought he would have deferred to his brother Edward IV. Gloucester resembled his father the duke of York more than Edward IV or George of Clarence, being a smallish dark man. Philippe de Commynes, the French historian, an exact contemporary, who had actually seen Richard, relates that Louis XI, a crafty king of France, thought Richard 'extremely cruel and evil'. He killed Henry VI or at least had him killed in his presence. In his estimate of Richard's character, More had the advantage of having served in his boyhood in the household of John Morton, sometime bishop of Ely, and would have benefitted from the fact that Morton had known Richard and had knowledge of events.

Richard III has had many defenders, both in the past and present, none more than his champion Sir Clements Markham, who published a book in 1906 even accusing Henry VII of the murder of the princes in the Tower. In his accusation, Markham never provided the slightest proof that Henry Tudor was guilty of such a crime, though he attempts to prove that the detailed story of the murder can, at least in part, be made to fit the beginning of Henry VII's reign better than that of Richard III. It is fair to add that Markham could not have benefitted from Mancini's observations because the Italian work was published in its present form in 1936.

Lord Stanley, Henry Tudor's stepfather, Morton bishop of Ely, and William Lord Hastings were among the counsellors assembled in the White Tower on 13 June 1483. Lord Hastings had been Edward IV's most intimate friend, both on the battlefield and in their amatory adventures. Hastings had also been friends with Richard. As he was absolutely loyal to the father, so might he be expected to be devoted to the interests of Edward V, the boy king, and the duke of York. More wrote vividly thus:

> It was nine o'clock, a day of summer, when the Lord Protector entered the room, apologizing courteously to the company for keeping them waiting, and addressing the Bishop of Ely, 'My lord, you have very good strawberries at your garden in Holberne, I require you let us have a messe of them'. Morton hastened to comply. Richard returned to the Council Chamber in a very different mood an hour later with a wonderful soure angrye countenance, knitting the browes, frowning and froting and knawing on hys lippes.

> There followed a scene when the Lord Protector showed the bewildered lords his withered arm, telling them that Edward's Queen and his mistress Mrs. Shore had bewitched him. When Hastings tried to argue, Richard cried: 'What! Thou servest me, I ween, with iffes and with andes. I tell thee they have so done ...' And anon the Protector said to the bewildered Hastings: 'I arrest the Traitour'. Somebody cried 'Treason' and men in harness rushed into the Chamber. In the prevailing confusion, somebody struck the Lord Stanley, who fell under the table 'or els his hed had been clefte to the tethe'. 'By Saynt Poule', cried Richard, 'I wil not to dinner til I se thy hed of.'[2]

So this nobleman was butchered on a log of wood in the Tower and his body buried beside Edward IV.

The fifteenth century was a very superstitious age, full of omens and most people were influenced by dreams and predictions. Lord Stanley the night before Lord Hastings's death had a fearful dream in which 'a boar with his tusks so raced them both bi the heddes, that the blood ran about both their shoulders'. The boar was the Protector's cognisaunce. Stanley sent a trusty messenger to warn his friend, but Hastings poured scorn on the matter, saying that it was plain witchcraft to believe in such dreams.

As a pretext for usurping his nephew's throne, Richard claimed that his own mother, the duchess of York, had committed adultery and that Edward and George were consequently bastards. He claimed to be the only legitimate member of his family.

On Sunday 22 June – the day on which Edward V was supposed to be crowned – Dr. Ralph Shaa (Shaw), a brother of the goldsmith Lord Mayor of London, a popular preacher, took as his text in his sermon at St. Paul's Cross near St. Paul's Cathedral: 'Bastard slips shall not take deep root'. There was an ominous silence. He claimed Edward IV's marriage to

Elizabeth Woodville invalid because he had been previously betrothed to Lady Eleanor Butler.

Dominic Mancini, a scholarly Italian eyewitness, was in London during 1483 and later wrote his manuscript of the *De occupatione regni anglie per Ricardum Tercium*.[3] His account is especially invaluable when he tells of the demeanour of the people at this time: Edward V never to be crowned and 'little prating York' were still in the royal apartments in the Tower (then a palace as well as a prison), but they were removed to the Garden Tower (now the Bloody Tower since the reign of James I) after 25 June, a short time before Richard's crowning as King of England. Let Mancini take up the tale:

> After Hastings was removed, all the attendants, who had waited upon the King were debarred access to him. He and his brother were withdrawn into the inner apartments of the Tower proper, and day by day began to be seen more rarely behind the bars and windows till at length they ceased to appear altogether ... I have seen many men burst forth into tears and lamentations when mention was made of him after his removal from men's sight.

Already there was a suspicion that he had been done away with.

Mancini left England for France shortly after Richard III's coronation, finishing his study of Richard's usurpation on 1 December (1483) at Beaugency. Later when Henry of Richmond came to the throne as Henry VII, men expressed astonishment that Henry had preserved a discreet silence concerning the fate of the princes, leading to an altogether unjustified suspicion that he himself was responsible for their deaths. There was a very good reason for Henry's reticence. He was only too well aware of the views about English kingship expressed by the kings of France, Louis XI and Charles VIII. Intending to lend dignity and authority to the English crown now that he was married to Elizabeth of York, sister of the murdered princes, he was unwilling to damage the kingdom by evil publicity abroad.

Mancini praises Edward V highly for his scholarly attainments and his liberal education. In his work he refers to Edward's last attendant to be left with him, his physician Dr. John Argentine,[4] who treated the wretched young prince for toothache. Argentine reported that the prince, like a victim prepared for sacrifice, sought remission of his sins, by daily confession and penance because he believed that death was confronting him. It is interesting that Henry VII, after 1485, chose this learned man as physician to his eldest son Prince Arthur and must when conversing with him have alluded to those lamentable times.

The mother of the princes in the Tower had gone into sanctuary at Westminster, the guest of the abbot of Westminster Abbey.

Nobody played such an important part as Henry Stafford, second duke of Buckingham, in raising Richard to the throne. He was very conscious of the royal blood in his veins, being directly descended from Thomas of Woodstock, youngest son of Edward III and from John of Gaunt. Extremely ambitious and proud, a very persuasive speaker, and handsome in appearance, he possessed much magnetism and charm. Immensely wealthy since he owned vast estates in Brecon and elsewhere, he hankered for more, the enormous Bohun estates. He suffered from a perpetual sense of grievance that he had been deliberately excluded from office by Edward IV. Forced to marry Catherine Woodville, a member of the queen's family, he deeply resented his marriage, for he probably remained a secret Lancastrian in his sympathies.

King Richard III and his Queen Anne Neville – younger daughter of the earl of Warwick and formerly the wife of Edward of Lancaster – were crowned in Westminster Abbey on 16 July 1483 by old Cardinal Bourchier, who showed his disapproval by staying away from the coronation banquet.[5] Richard was dressed in a magnificent doublet of blue cloth of gold, wearing over it a purple velvet gown trimmed with ermine. To outmatch him, Harry Buckingham wore a robe of blue velvet embroidered with blazing golden cartwheels.

One would like to have known Henry Tudor's mother's thoughts as the chief bearer of Queen Anne of Warwick's train, who was wearing a gorgeous gown of crimson velvet. At the altar the Lady Stanley (Countess of Richmond in her own right) stood on the queen's left. Her husband, after his arrest in the Tower, had been restored to Richard's favour. He was not only Steward of the Household but High Constable of England, having agreed to support the usurper king. The duke of Buckingham carried the king's train, but he showed his disgust at the moment of crowning by turning his head aside.

Yet he had been handsomely rewarded by Richard becoming Lord Great Chamberlain and Knight of the Garter, among other high offices. The king, too, gave him the remainder of the Bohun estates. People were increasingly disenchanted with Richard III, disapproving his usurpation of his nephew's throne. Buckingham's rebellion about fifteen weeks after Richard's coronation was to have a powerful influence on Henry Tudor's fortunes, making him a possible rival, as an alternative ruler for many Lancastrian supporters and for those Yorkists discontented with Richard's seizure of the throne. His motives for turning against Richard are rather obscure. Personal ambition may have played a part, for Henry Stafford could sense Richard's increasing lack of popularity. He may have fancied himself in the role of king.

Richard unwisely had committed to Buckingham's custody John Morton after his arrest on 13 June. The bishop of Ely was taken to Buckingham's magnificent castle at Brecknock (Brecon), and Sir Thomas More tells us that there 'waxed with him familiar'.[6]

Morton was extremely intelligent and wily, 'a man of great natural wit, very wel lerned, and honorable in behaveor, lacking no wise wiles to win favor'.[7] Gairdner, the author of a biography of King Richard, wrote of Morton as 'a man possessed of great qualities for the crooked times in which he lived'. Born in 1420, he was now sixty-three. Far from being a turncoat, he had suffered much for the cause of Lancaster, serving Henry VI and his queen Margaret of Anjou with loyalty and devotion. He had been present in York with Henry and Margaret during the savage Battle of Towton and may have fought there. The Lancastrians had suffered terrible carnage. Henry and Margaret had fled to Scotland where Morton was among their followers and later, when the intrepid queen was in desperate straits living the life of a fugitive at the Castle of Koeur-la-Petite, owned by her father King René in the duchy of Bar, Morton remained in exile.[8] There is no doubt that, whilst in his custody, Bishop Morton worked on Buckingham, weaning him away from allegiance to King Richard and influencing him to correspond with Henry Tudor.

He told Buckingham:

If the worlde woold have gone as I would have wished King Henryes sonne had had the crown and not King Edward. But after that God had ordered hym to lese it, I was never so mad, that I would with a dead man strive against the quicke...

So he became King Edward IV's faithful chaplain and Edward had rewarded him with high office.

The contemporary historian Polydore Vergil later gave the Lady Margaret Stanley, Countess of Richmond, a very active role as instigator of the conspiracy of Harry Stafford, duke of Buckingham. She was a very shrewd, 'wise woman', as Vergil admitted, harbouring always thoughts how her son's fortunes might be improved. She pondered long. If Henry's chance to succeed to the throne might ensue, it would be vital for him to take in marriage, Elizabeth, eldest daughter of Edward IV and Queen Elizabeth Woodville, now in sanctuary at Westminster. The Lady Margaret discussed this matter in deep secrecy with her Welsh-born physician, Dr. Lewis Caerleon, who happened also to be Queen Elizabeth's physician. It is unlikely that Margaret would have acted in such a way unless she shared a belief with many people, that the death of King Edward's two sons had occurred during the late summer (1483) in the Tower.

Dr. Lewis was favourably received by Queen Elizabeth, who agreed to the scheme, promising that she would persuade all her friends to support Henry Tudor, provided he would swear he would marry Elizabeth, or if she should die, her younger daughter Cecily. Margaret trusted none of the officials serving her more than her Receiver-General Reginald Bray, who was now sent to Brecon where in deep secrecy he recruited a large number of conspirators. To Henry in Brittany, she resolved to send a trusty priest named Christopher Urswick, followed by another messenger Hugh Conway, who had 'more reputation and credit' than Urswick. Conway was given a considerable sum of money for Henry's use and told to encourage him to land in Wales as part of the insurrection. Lady Margaret possessed immense political skill and it was masterly to make use of Buckingham as political cover for her son's ambition.

Sir George Buck,[9] the early seventeenth century antiquary, a Yorkist in sympathy, is very hostile to Margaret Beaufort and critical of her political activity. To him she was a very sinister character, dubbing her a 'politic and subtle lady' by whose malign influence Henry, duke of Buckingham was induced to head the rebellion against Richard III. Buck makes the absurd accusation that she and her chaplain John Morton were involved in a plot with others to cause the deaths by sorcery and poison of the princes in the Tower. His case was founded on very slight evidence, an old manuscript book which was never produced. Another critic, Sir William Cornwallis, thought Richard III foolish for failing to deal with her more drastically, having her executed instead of merely having her kept in close custody by her husband Lord Stanley. He considered it a weakness in his rule leading to his fall.

There were risings planned at Brecon, Salisbury, Newbury in Berkshire and Gravesend in Kent. A band of rebels in Surrey and Kent intended to march on London and join the duke of Buckingham's army as it approached from Wales. Richard III was in Lincoln when he received news of the rebellion. He immediately wrote to Dr. Russell, bishop of Lincoln, the Chancellor, charging him to send him the Great Seal and summoning him to his presence, but Russell was ill and unable to travel. Richard wrote to him, that he had no chance of being unable to defeat 'the malice of him that had best cause to be true, the duke of Buckingham, the most untrue creature living'.

Buckingham, with his forces, wishing to cross into England from Wales, was prevented by the atrocious weather that October. Torrential rain fell, causing severe flooding and the Severn to overflow. For long this was known as 'The Duke of Buckingham's water'. His men, drenched to the skin and starving, deserted him, while John Morton, resourceful as ever, fled in disguise to the Fens and escaped to Flanders. Buckingham was probably betrayed by a servant named Ralph Bannister, lured by the promised reward of money. However, according to the author of *The Continuation of the Chronicle of Croyland*, Buckingham was 'discovered disguised in the cottage of a poor man', in consequence of a greater quantity of provisions than usual being carried there. He was taken to Salisbury, to be tried and executed on 2 November in the marketplace, though he attempted to obtain an interview with Richard, which was never granted.

Henry Tudor set forth from Brittany with some misgivings, but hopefully because Duke Francis had agreed to advance him a loan of 10,000 crowns. Records of this transaction can be seen in the British Library.[10] The duke had instructed his auditors to allow the Treasurer of his Exchequer the money if required. Henry sailed to England with 5,000 men in 15 ships. The date is uncertain. Possibly on 19 October when he was attainted, or later. Ill fortune attended the expedition, because of vile weather, causing most of the ships to be driven back to Normandy or Brittany. The ship bearing Henry and another ship arrived either at Poole harbour, according to Polydore Vergil, or Plymouth as mentioned later in the act of attainder. The author of *The Continuation of the Chronicle of Croyland* also alludes to Plymouth.

Henry very wisely, for adversity had taught him caution and secrecy, refused to land or allow his men to disembark. Seeing many soldiers on the coast, seemingly ready to welcome him, pretending that they supported Buckingham, Henry instinctively distrusted them, fearing they were Richard III's soldiers come to arrest him. He ordered his crew to hoist sail and returned via Normandy to Brittany, where he first heard of the duke of Buckingham's execution. Louis XI had died on 30 August 1483, so Henry sought permission from his son, the boy king Charles VIII to pass through Normandy to Brittany. Charles not only granted his permission but sent his good wishes.

The rebellion had been a dismal failure, but there were beneficial repercussions. A large number of fugitives arrived in Vannes to join Henry, including the marquess of Dorset, a son of Queen Elizabeth Woodville by her first marriage and Edward Woodville.

King Richard's parliament, assembling at Westminster during January to February 1484, attainted as many as 104 people, convicting them of high treason. Henry, calling himself earl of Richmond, and Jasper, calling himself earl of Pembroke, were convicted for their part in planning the insurrection at Brecon, together with four others. As might be expected, John Morton, bishop of Ely, was attainted, as were Lionel Woodville, bishop of Salisbury, and Peter Courtenay, bishop of Exeter. Attainder resulted in a man's possessions being forfeited.

Among those who fled into exile in Brittany were Peter Courtenay, bishop of Exeter, Edward Courtenay, earl of Devonshire, Thomas Grey, marquess of Dorset as already mentioned, and Thomas his son, John Bourchier, John Welles (later to marry Cecily, Elizabeth of York's younger sister), Edward Woodville, Giles Daubeny, Robert Willoughby, John Cheyney and his two brothers, William Brandon and his brother, Thomas, Richard Edgecombe and Evan Morgan of a leading Welsh family. Many of these were to give Henry Tudor very useful service when he became king. Nobody exceeded John Morton in his support for Henry of Richmond, warning him on one occasion when his life was in deadly danger, but he chose to remain in Flanders rather than to come to Brittany. Another important recruit was Richard Fox, who joined Henry's cause later whilst studying at the university in Paris. A man of great ability, Fox was to prosper under the Tudors becoming Keeper of the Privy Purse, bishop of Exeter, of Bath and Wells, of Durham and of Winchester for twenty-seven years. He was a born negotiator.

King Richard did not treat Margaret, Countess of Richmond, mother to the king's great rebel with the utmost severity. Her husband, the Lord Stanley, was one of the most powerful persons in the realm, whom Richard no doubt did not want to antagonize more than necessary, for he considered him a prop to his throne and depended on him. However, it is likely that Thomas Stanley bore secret resentment against Richard in the light of his future behaviour. She was never attainted but accused of high treason, especially for sending messages, writings and tokens to Henry, stirring him to come into the country to make war. She was mainly charged with conspiring and imagining the destruction of the king and for asserting and assisting Henry duke of Buckingham in treason.[11] Her political sense told her exactly how far to go in her intrigues against Richard III. All her estates were transferred to her husband and she was disabled by law from having or inheriting land. Stanley was ordered to keep a rigid watch over her, but he took no steps to prevent her from corresponding with her beloved son. Their marriage had been one of policy and convenience rather than of real affection.

The possibility of a marriage between Henry Tudor and the eldest daughter of Edward IV, Elizabeth of York, had been broached over a year before the events of 1483. It is known that Lord Stanley and the Lady Margaret, often at Court, had discussed with Edward and Bishop Morton such a marriage and that a royal pardon for Henry exists written on the back of the patent that had created his father Edmund earl of Richmond.[12] Actually Edward, as his reign progressed, became eager for Elizabeth to make a dynastic marriage with the Dauphin of France, but the negotiations eventually came to nothing.

King Richard was anxious, if possible, to get Henry Tudor into his power. In July 1483 he sent Thomas Hutton, his confidential agent, an able, witty man to Brittany to negotiate with Duke Francis concerning the settlement of maritime questions, the chief bone of contention between England and the duchy. Henry's position in exile was certainly raised. Francis informed Richard that Louis XI while alive had continually pressed him to surrender Henry. He required more military assistance, 4,000 archers, to be supplied within a month of requesting them and 2,000 or 3,000 more within a further month. Though Henry's circumstances had been immensely strengthened by the Lancastrians, his natural supporters and disillusioned Yorkists fleeing what might be described as his rival court, he remained a pawn subject to bargaining.

Though favourably disposed towards Henry, the duke of Brittany suffered from feeble health and his intellectual ability was mediocre. He had two daughters, but no male heirs. Moreover, Brittany was proud of her independence from France and wanted to retain it. She had her own language, her own laws and institutions, and her old traditions meant everything to her. She was not interested in sending any representatives to the French estates.[13]

Charles VIII had succeeded to the throne of France at the age of thirteen, a boy king possessing indifferent health, and because of it had been made by his father, Louis XI, to live in strict seclusion in Amboise. He was very much under the domination of his elder sister Anne of Beaujeu aged twenty-two, one of the Regents, and a very capable, determined character. She very much resembled her father, purged of his defects, his cruelty and native cunning and hypocrisy, but she possessed his sense of authority[14]. Louis had, in his cynical fashion, said of his daughter that she was not the least foolish member of a sex, which contained no wise ones, while Brantôme, the French historian described her as '*le vrai image en tout du roy Louis son père*'. Her ambition was to annex Brittany, sparing no pains to ensure that the duchy should become part of the kingdom of France.

On Christmas Day 1483 when Henry was in Rennes with all his followers, mostly refugees who had fled to Brittany, they all sallied forth to the Cathedral where there was a sudden hush as Henry rose to speak. He was now almost twenty-six, a young man, vigorous and determined, schooled in adversity and danger. He made a solemn vow to return victorious to England and marry the Princess Elizabeth of York.[15] One by one, his followers approached to pledge their loyalty, while shouts of 'Henry, Henry' rose in the sacred precincts. Henry had learnt the necessity of patience.

Richard in London now took Henry Tudor as a rival very seriously indeed. To guard against the danger of future invasions, he adopted a practice first used by Edward IV. This was to station a single horseman every 20 miles along major roadways. When warnings were given, each man would ride as quickly as possible to the next point, an ingenious way of carrying letters from hand to hand 200 miles within two days.[16] In counties bordering the sea, beacons were lit on the top of every hill, ensuring that at any warning of danger, lights would flash arousing the people and alerting them to the necessity of defending themselves. In Brittany, Richard employed many spies ready to report the suspicious activities of Henry of Richmond.

Elizabeth of York was not only beautiful but a gentle character, thoughtful for others, and a source of strength to her younger sisters and mother. Her life had been saddened by tragedy. To gain his bloody ends, her uncle Richard had saddled her grandmother Cecily, the duchess of York, with the false accusation of adultery, so that both her father Edward IV and uncle George, duke of Clarence were illegitimate sons of the duke of York. Elizabeth had been the favourite daughter of her father,[17] who had been always willing to listen to the predictions of astrologers. Englishmen were very prone to it in that age.

The Song of the Lady Bessy, a metrical narrative, written by Humphrey Brereton, a vassal of the Lord Stanley, tells a strange story, neither history nor authentic, yet there may be a substance of truth in it. Her father was fond of books of magic and one day taking her on his lap told her of a prediction that no son of his would wear the crown after him, but that she would be queen and that her descendants would reign after her.

> For there shall never be son of my body begotten,
> That shall be crowned after me,
> But you shall be Queen and wear the crown,
> So doth express the prophecy.[18]

If Pierre Landois, the Duke Francis's Treasurer in Brittany, had succeeded in handing over Henry Tudor to King Richard, it is certain that Elizabeth would never have been his queen. Landois was temporarily at the head of government during part of the summer (1484) when Francis was incapacited by mental illness. For some time Richard had been urging Brittany to surrender Henry without success, but on 26 June he agreed to supply her with 1,000 archers for use in the defence of the duchy. Landois was very unpopular in Brittany and thought by yielding to the king's blandishments he would not only improve the poor relations between the duchy and England, but acquire Richard's support in the minister's quarrels with the Breton nobility.

Fortunately for Henry, Dr. John Morton in Flanders, whether at Bruges or Antwerp, became aware of the plot. By what means it is difficult to say, but he had many spies and agents and was in touch with the Countess of Stanley (Lady Margaret Beaufort) in England. It may be that Lord Stanley, who regularly attended meetings of the Council, heard of it, and immediately informed his wife. Morton then sent Christopher Urswick to Brittany to urge Henry to leave immediately and to advise him to escape to France. Having performed his mission, Urswick hastened to France to obtain a safe conduct for Henry to enter France. He acted with the deepest secrecy, only confiding in Uncle Jasper. Escaping with his servants and after exchanging clothes with them in a wood, he rode hard on the lesser roads (one wonders what state they were in). Guided by one of them, he safely arrived on the borders of Anjou. A desperate adventure, for Landois on hearing of his escape, had sent out men-at-arms in pursuit.

When the French Council of Regency heard on 11 October of Henry's safe arrival, they ordered that he should receive a suitable welcome and financial resources provided for him and his party.[19] They regarded him as a valuable pawn in their relations with England and Brittany.

When Duke Francis recovered from his illness, he was very angry at the duplicity of Landois. However, he showed good sense and generosity by sending for Edward Poynings and Edward Woodville, two of Henry's close friends. After giving them adequate money for the journey, he told them to escort all the remaining followers, consisting of 300 persons, to rejoin Henry in France. Henry never forgot his debt to Francis. He now calculated that his chances of a successful invasion of England largely depended on France. Would he get enough support from her to make his plans possible? The Council of Regency might well help him if they were able to embarrass Richard III and prevent him from going to the aid of Brittany in the forthcoming struggle of the last of the independent duchies against France. They were also aware that the Austrian Hapsburg Archduke Maxmilian, then Regent of the Netherlands for his son Philip, viewed the French policy of acquiring Brittany with apprehension and dismay.

IV   EVENTS LEADING TO BOSWORTH

During early 1484 Richard was becoming increasingly unpopular. He possessed none of his brother Edward's easy ways, and lacked for the most part the spark that kindles affection and promotes love. However, in parts of the northern kingdom, especially in York, he was genuinely loved. But he was also feared as a tyrant, never trusted and suspected by many of the murder of his nephews. True, hardly anybody dared to mention it. Yet Richard was an efficient king. He tried to rule wisely, and denied the right of any king to be able to demand money directly from his countrymen. That was a matter for parliament. It was for them to levy taxes and declare the uses to which the money would be put. In the courts of law, jurors should be qualified and impartial, allowing defendants the right to bail. He also showed energy in quelling piracies on the high seas.

When parliament assembled on 22 January 1484, 'after frequent entreaties as well as threats had been made use of', according to the author of *The Continuation of the Croyland Chronicle*, Queen Elizabeth sent all her daughters from the sanctuary at Westminster to King Richard. *The Croyland Chronicle* is acknowledged today as being probably the work of John Russell, bishop of Lincoln. The five daughters were Elizabeth, now a beautiful girl, almost nineteen, Cecily, Anne, Katherine and Bridget.

The queen's agreement to comply with the wishes of her brother-in-law, the king, has been used as an argument by those who refuse to believe that she knew Richard was the murderer of her two sons. However, the queen was not of strong character, prepared to sacrifice herself or her family. She had grown tired of the austere, monotonous and isolated conditions she had had to endure in Westminster, though kindly treated by Abbot Eastney and the monks of the Abbey. Her decision does not infer that she considered Richard guiltless of his crimes. It would seem that she no longer had implicit faith that Henry Tudor would return from overseas to deliver her and her daughters from their woes. So, she wrote miserably to her son by her first marriage, the marquess of Dorset, to abandon Henry's cause and come home to make his peace with Richard III, since he seemed secure enough on his throne. Dorset attempted to come home, but was prevented by Henry's agents.

The king swore an oath before an assemblage of lords, spiritual and temporal, and of the Lord Mayor and Aldermen, that if the daughters of Dame Elizabeth Grey, 'late calling herself Queen of England', would come to him out of the sanctuary of Westminster, and be ruled and guided by him, he would, he promised, 'see that they be in surety of their lives...' He further undertook that 'such gentleman as shall hap to marry with them, I shall strictly charge lovingly to love and entreat them, as wives and my kinswomen...'[1]

One son only, Edward, had been born to Anne Neville, Richard's delicate queen. The birth had taken place in 1474 at Middleham in Yorkshire, where they lived as duke and duchess of Gloucester. As Richard wanted his son to be acknowledged as his heir 'and supreme lord' if anything should happen to him, he commanded the lords of the realm, both spiritual and temporal together with 'higher knights' and esquires to attend a ceremony in a lower room near the queen's, during February (1484), in the palace apartments of Westminster.[2] Each person had to take an oath of adherence to Prince Edward. John Howard, recently created duke of Norfolk, was the nobleman of highest rank to swear in such a way. He was always loyal to Richard III as he subsequently proved at Bosworth.

It was all in vain. Edward was in delicate health, much like his mother, and suddenly 'seized with an illness of but short duration' he died aged about ten at Middleham Castle. Richard and Anne were residing in Nottingham Castle when they heard the dreadful news. 'You might have seen his father and mother in a state almost bordering on madness, by reason of their sudden grief,' wrote the author of *The Croyland Chronicle*. Edward Plantagenet died on 9 April 1484.

We know little enough about Richard's marriage with Anne. He may have at first cared for her in the early days at Middleham, but she was a great heiress as was her elder sister Isabel and this also would have counted with him.

Richard's nearest heir was Edward, earl of Warwick, his nephew, son of his brother George and Isabel. As he had named George of Clarence a bastard, this wretched half-witted boy was hardly suitable to be nominated his successor and heir presumptive. Another candidate was found, John de la Pole, earl of Lincoln, son of another John, duke of Suffolk, and of Elizabeth Plantagenet and sister of Edward IV.

Christmas 1484 was a very gay season at court. It may be that Richard instinctively felt it was his last. In the midst of the splendour and the gaiety he received ominous messages that his enemy Henry Tudor and his adversaries were preparing to invade the kingdom during the following summer.

It was obvious to many people that Richard was much attracted by the beauty and grace of his niece the Princess Elizabeth. People murmured because she and the queen wore dresses of very similar mould and shape. It was known that Richard had tired of Anne, particularly as she could no longer bear him an infant prince. It was whispered that he intended to divorce her or even to poison her, so that he would be free to marry Princess Elizabeth. Almost certainly he was tempted. Such a marriage would thwart the dynastic ambitions of his rival Henry, whose own claims to kingship lay on slender foundations, although he was the Lancastrian heir.

Anne's own life may have been shortened by knowing what was going on in her husband's mind. Anyhow, the queen felt extremely sick and died on 16 March 1485. For some time before her death, the king had completely shunned her bed, declaring that it was owing to the advice of his physicians.[3]

Richard could hardly have harboured thoughts of marriage with Elizabeth for long because his own title depended on his declaration of the bastardy of Edward IV's children. Besides, many people would have been horrified that Richard would be committing incest by marrying his niece. Those fears were even voiced by two of his intimate advisers, William Catesby and Richard Ratcliffe. They warned the king that if he persisted in his intention even his loyal northern subjects would rebel against him.

In France Henry Tudor was deeply troubled by the rumours, which he believed to be true. 'They pinched him to the very stomach,' alleged Polydore Vergil in a memorable phrase. Henry naturally feared that unless he married Elizabeth of York or one of her sisters, large droves of his supporters would desert him.

In his dilemma he consulted some of his friends, who advised him to negotiate a marriage with Walter Herbert's sister. He was a younger son of Henry's former guardian William Herbert earl of Pembroke and brother of the present earl, who lacked his father's ambition and was inactive. Maud Herbert, whom he had originally been intended to marry, had since been wedded to Henry Percy, fourth earl of Northumberland. She died during the summer (1485).

Walter had much influence with the Welsh and it was hoped that this would attract them to Henry's cause. A message from Henry to the Herberts was intercepted, which was fortunate for him because he soon heard that Richard would not marry Elizabeth of York. Though he wavered, Walter may have come to Henry's aid before Bosworth. After the battle the Herberts, no longer Yorkists, served the Tudor.

Ratcliffe and Catesby advised King Richard to summon the Mayor of London and citizens to the hall of the Knights of St. John at Clerkenwell where he was forced to deny in a 'loud and distinct voice' that he had ever intended to marry his niece. Nor had he poisoned Queen Anne, so as to be free to do so. There were some members of the Council who suspected that the contrary was true.[4] Twelve doctors of divinity were also prepared to say that the Pope could grant no dispensation in a case of such a close degree of consanguinity.

Ratcliffe and Catesby were very unpopular. One day during July 1484, two lines of verse were found nailed to the door of St. Paul's:

> The Rat, the Cat, the Lovell[5] our dog
> Rule all England under the Hog.

Meanwhile, Henry wrote constantly from France to important potential supporters.

What did Elizabeth of York herself think of this proposed match with Richard? She was already betrothed to Henry Tudor. According to Grafton in his continuation of More's *History of Richard III*, 'the maiden abhorred this unlawful desire as a thing most detestable'. Sir George Buck, however, a strong Yorkist partisan writing during the early seventeenth century, claims to have seen among the Howard papers in the cabinet of the earl of Arundel, a letter from the princess to the duke of Norfolk saying 'the King was her joy and maker in this world, and that she was his in heart and thought'. He alleges that she was surprised at the duration of the queen's sickness and that she would never die: Buck is not to be trusted. There is no corroborative testimony that this letter was ever written and what we know of Elizabeth makes it almost impossible to conceive that it was her work. It might well be, however, that her mother would not have put any insuperable obstacle in their way. When he had ascertained that marriage with her was impossible, Richard sent Elizabeth of York to his castle of Sheriff Hutton in Yorkshire out of the way of Henry Tudor where her only companion was the imbecile earl of Warwick.

For Henry Tudor the summer of 1485 was a period of uncertainty and deep worry. He knew not whom he could rely on or indeed whom he could trust. He was 'ravished with joy' according to Polydore Vergil when John de Vere, thirteenth earl of Oxford, succeeded in escaping from Hammes Castle near Calais where he had been imprisoned for ten years. John de Vere was the son of the twelfth earl, who had been executed by Edward IV. He was from a family that had been consistently loyal to the cause of Lancaster and indeed suffered for it. Oxford had fought with valour at Barnet (1471). It was no fault of his that the Lancastrians had sustained a decisive defeat. He was a highly experienced, gifted soldier on whom Henry could count on organizing his army and he brought with him two valuable recruits, James Blunt, the Captain at Hammes Castle, and Sir John Fortescue, the gentleman porter of Calais.

Henry Tudor was little known in England up to 1485. Many sympathized with his cause, but dared not avow it. What he desperately needed was the open support of the most powerful people in the realm, such as the Stanleys. He constantly wrote to his friends. A typical letter is the following:

> Being given to understand your good devour and entreaty to advance me to the furtherance of my rightful claim, due and lineal inheritance of that crown and for the just depriving of that homicidal and unnatural tyrant, which now unjustly bears dominion over you, I give you to understand that no Christian heart can be more full of joy than the heart of me your poor exiled friend, who will, upon the instant of your sure advertising what power you will make ready and what captains and leaders you get to conduct, be prepared to pass over the sea with such force as my friends here are preparing for me. And if you have such good speed and success as I wish according to your desire, I shall ever be most forward to remember and wholly to requite this your most loving kindness in my just quarrel. H.R.

Henry sometimes before becoming king signed himself Henricus Rex.[6]

Richard retaliated during June 1485 with a proclamation against 'Piers Courtenay, bishop of Exeter, Jasper Tudor, son of Owen Tudor, calling himself earl of Pembroke, John late earl of Oxford and Sir Richard Woodville with other divers rebels and traitours...'[7] His strongest abuse was left for:

> one Henry Tydder, son of Edward Tydder, son of Owen Tydder, which of his ambitiousness, and insatiable covetise encroacheth and usurpeth upon him the name and title of royal estate of this realm of England, whereunto he has no manner, interest, right, title or colour, as every man well knoweth. For he is descended of bastard blood, both of father side and of mother side, for the said Owen the grandfather was bastard born, and his mother was daughter unto John Duke of Somerset son unto John Earl of Somerset, son unto Dame Katherine Swynford, and of their double adultery.

In France Henry had an interview with Charles VIII, the young king of France, at Angers. He claimed to be rightful King of England, telling Charles that the nobility were calling on him to return to his kingdom. The people loathed the tyranny of Richard III. Charles told Henry that he was well disposed towards him, but at this stage gave him little practical help.

However, Anne of Beaujeu was the most influential member of the government, being married to Pierre de Bourbon, Lord of Beaujeu and heir to the duchy of Bourbon. Henry continued to press her for essential funds to finance his expedition, and she eventually agreed to lend him 40,000 livres. Two sureties, Lord Dorset who had upset Henry by his attempted return to England, and John Bourchier were left in custody in France until the money was repaid. Friends in England advanced him additional funds. Henry's army consisted of about 3,000 men, composed of, perhaps, 500 followers from Brittany consisting of Welsh and English. Many were Cornish. Joining his forces was a French contingent commanded by a Breton Philibert de Chandée, later created by Henry VII, earl of Bath. There were also some mercenaries and others without military experience.

At the height of summer, it seems probable that Henry's men brought with them from France a devastating disease known as the English sweating sickness of *sudor anglicus*. It struck suddenly. A man could be healthy one day, short of breath the next and dead the following. Mention of it is made in *The Croyland Chronicle*[8] during 1484:

> For behold! On a sudden, the plague or sweating sickness, made great ravages, and in a few days, in the City of London destroyed two mayors and four or five aldermen, besides many members of the highest and most wealthy classes in other parts of the country.

Among its victims was Lambert Fossedyke, the well-loved Abbot of Croyland Monastery, during the very early reign of Henry VII. Lord Stanley either pretended or really was suffering from the disease when he made it an excuse for not joining King Richard at Nottingham, when summoned for that purpose before Bosworth. The king distrusted Stanley, fearing not without reason that the Lady Margaret, his wife, would go over to the party of her son. However, Stanley had been given permission to visit his estates in Lancashire. Richard now insisted that his son by his first marriage, Lord Strange, should be left as hostage and kept under close guard. According to *The Croyland Chronicle*, George Strange tried to desert, 'but was detected by stratagem'. He was forced to confess that together with his uncle Sir William Stanley and Sir John Savage, he had been planning to desert to Henry Tudor. It was made plain to Lord Stanley that his son's life depended on his father's behaviour.

If some of his most influential commanders had not proved treacherous, Richard should have defeated Henry at Bosworth, for his army was composed of 10,000-15,000 men, mounted archers and men-at-arms. Henry's forces were, perhaps, 5,000, so they were heavily outnumbered. Richard used cannons, known as 'serpentines', which were light guns and could be transported rapidly in fast carts.[9] There is evidence that Henry also used cannon and artillery at Bosworth, provided for him in France according to Commynes, but he may also have taken some pieces from Tamworth Castle, whose owner was the Yorkist Sir Thomas Ferrers. Ferrers was the brother-in-law of Lord Hastings, and consequently his sentiments towards Richard were far from amicable.

Before Henry sailed from Harfleur, he received an encouraging message from one of his supporters in Wales, John Morgan of Tredegar, that Rhys ap Thomas, a source of power in Wales, and John Savage would openly support him. Yet Henry remained doubtful and apprehensive as to his reception in Wales and especially in England. He sailed with, perhaps, 2,300 men in a few ships, under better auspices than the unsuccessful expedition of October 1483, because on Monday 1 August 1485 there was a favourable soft southern wind. It was wise of Henry to choose landing at a secluded harbour, Mill Bay off Milford Haven on the west coast of Pembrokeshire, since Uncle Jasper had many friends there. To land in Wales took Richard by surprise, uncertain of his rival's movements, he only heard of his landing later.

On setting foot on earth a little before sunset on Sunday 7 August, Henry kissed Welsh soil reciting in Latin the verse from the Psalms: 'Be thou my judge, O Lord, for I have walked innocently.' He immediately created sixteen knights among his followers, including Edward Poynings, John Fortescue, and Edward Courtenay.

His anxieties remained intense for there was no rush to join his army. According to a family history, Henry was joined immediately by Rhys ap Thomas, the leading Welshman in the region, but it is not true. Anxious news reached Henry's camp, for a rumour spread as soon as he set out from Haverfordwest, that Walter Herbert and his followers in the town of Carmarthen were there with a huge army ready to resist him.[10] Henry Tudor sent out scouts who reported that 'all thyngs were quiet and that ther was no hindrance to their voyage immynent'.

Rhys was in a peculiarly difficult situation because for some time he had seemed to support Richard although the king did not trust him. When Richard had demanded that the Welshman should swear an oath of allegiance and send his son to him as a hostage, he had refused to obey the king, saying that his boy was only four years old. After the failure of the Buckingham Rebellion, Rhys had corresponded with Henry of Richmond and espoused his cause. Ultimately, Rhys attached himself to Henry, although he had once sworn to Richard that any Pretender would have 'to make entrance over his bellie'.

On through wild country moved Henry's army, through the Prescelly mountains and through Cardigan. It is almost certain that he did not receive an offer of Rhys's support until he reached Newport over a week after landing. There, on 15 August, he also received Gilbert Talbot, an uncle of the earl of Shrewsbury with welcome reinforcements of 500 men.[11] Polydore Vergil relates that Henry sent secret messages to his mother, to Lord Stanley and to his brother Sir William. When he reached Shrewsbury on 15 August, the town made a token of closing its gates.

To a Welshman John ap Meredith, Henry wrote on crossing the border into England:

> Right Trusty and well beloved, wee greete you well, and whereas it is soe, that through the helps of Almighty God, the assistance of our loving and true subjects, and the greate confidence that wee have to the nobles and commons of this our Principalities of Wales, we be entered into the same, purposing by the helpe above rehearsed, in all haste possible to descend into our realme of England, not only for the adoption of the Crowne, unto us of right appertaining, but also for the oppression of the tyrant Richard late Duke of Gloucester, usurper of our said rights and moreover to reduce as well our saide realme of England into its ancient estate, honour and property, and prosperitie as this our said principalitie of Wales.[12]

Henry is said to have stayed one night with Rhys ap Thomas at Crew Castle.

When Henry reached Stafford about 17 August, he had a short meeting with Sir William Stanley. What actually transpired is not known. Perhaps Sir William made vague promises of help during the forthcoming battle. The following day Henry met Lord Stanley and his brother at Atherstone near market Bosworth. More and more he came to realize that their help was vital.

Meanwhile on 19 August, Richard with his closest friends John duke of Norfolk, Viscount Lovel and others marched from Nottingham Castle to Leicester where his army was assembling. In Leicester, he installed himself in the White Boar Inn, a huge, rambling half-timbered building. Richard was a kingly figure, a hard-seasoned warrior, grim and determined as he rode his white charger. He was a very experienced soldier. On the other hand, Henry had no experience of warfare. On his head Richard wore a jewelled coronet, valued at £20,000. Despite all his appearance of splendour, Richard was a worried man, for Sir William Stanley, though he had been declared a traitor, was still with his brother and the king suspected that treachery was in the air.

One nobleman he summoned to Leicester was Henry Percy, fourth earl of Northumberland, wisely restored to his earldom by Edward IV, but now a secret enemy of Richard's, for he was in communication with Henry.

Richard certainly misjudged Northumberland's character. The Percies, during the reign of Henry VI, had been staunch adherents and had deeply suffered for it. The fourth earl had taken, however, a solemn oath to save Richard (his indenture is preserved in Alnwick Castle today), but a gnawing jealousy of the usurper king had been awakened by the king's popularity and pre-eminence in northern parts of his kingdom, and especially in the city of York. The proud Percies would brook no rival in the north-east where, employed as Lords Wardens, they enjoyed enormous prestige. His failure to support Richard at Bosworth can be traced to this sentiment.

On the night of 19 August, Henry unfortunately lost contact with his army while marching from Lichfield to Tamworth, and was compelled with 20 men to conceal himself in a village, fearful of being captured by Richard. Then they discovered they were only three miles from Tamworth and Henry was able to rejoin his army.

Henry Tudor spent Sunday 21 August near Atherstone, perhaps attending services and receiving hospitality at Merevale Abbey. His troops were out foraging for corn in the district and it is recorded that three months after the battle Henry repaid the villages of Atherstone, Witherly, Mancetter and Fenny Drayton for corn taken by his soldiers.[13] One useful adherent to his cause was a local man John de Hardwick, lord of the manor of Lindley, who came to Henry's camp the night before the battle with men and horses. As he had intimate knowledge of local topography, he was an invaluable recruit. Whether Henry on the night of 21 August encamped with his army at the White Moors, about a mile from Shenton in Leicestershire, is rather uncertain. Bosworth Field is about 15 miles from Leicester. On the road from Tamworth, eight miles from Lichfield in Staffordshire, Henry received fresh recruits. His army probably numbered not more than 5,000 men, while Richard's army was at least double that number. Henry remained in a state of tension, not dispelled when he sent an urgent message to Lord Stanley early in the morning of 22 August to come to his assistance. Stanley merely replied 'that the earl set his own men in good order of battle while he would array his company, and come to him in time convenient'.

When Richard, whose headquarters the night before Bosworth were at Sutton Cheney, two miles south of the village of Market Bosworth, sent a similar message to Stanley to join his forces, he categorically refused to comply. He was only too aware that his refusal would endanger the life of his son. Richard immediately ordered Lord Strange to be beheaded, but owing to the stress of preparing for the battle, the order was not carried out.

The chronicler Hall describes Henry as he stood on a hill to make an inspiring speech to his men: 'He was of no great stature, his countenance and aspecte was chereful and courageous, his heare yellow lyke the burnished golde, his eyes shynynge and quicke'. He described 'younder tyraunt Richard Duke of Gloucester ... which is both Tarquine and Nero'.

It was fortunate for the Lancastrians that their commander, the thirteenth earl of Oxford (John de Vere), was the best and most experienced soldier on either side. He led the vanguard, while Henry commanded the reserve, a troop of men-at-arms and a few archers and billmen; and some cavalry.

According to Polydore Vergil,[14] the night before the battle Richard had a terrible dream:

> for he thought in his slepe that he saw horryble ymages, as yt were of evell spyrtes haunting evydently about him, as yt were before his eyes ... which visyon trewly dyd not so much stryke into his brest a suddane feare, as replenyshe the same with heavy cares.

His haggard expression must have presented a ghastly sight for his followers on the following day. While sleeping, somebody had also stuck a note on Norfolk's tent containing the couplet:

> Jockey of Norfolk be not too bold
> For Dickon thy master is bought and sold.

An unfavourable omen for the superstitious!

It is difficult to reconstruct exactly what happened on August 22 at Bosworth, which was a marsh in 1485. Richard's frontline troops, positioned on the western slopes of Ambion Hill, opened the attack on Henry's men who had reached the end of the marsh below. His four-pounders opened fire very effectively, but owing to having to attack down the slope were not as accurate as they might have been. Then raising a great cry, 8,000 of Norfolk's men charged down the hill letting loose a deadly flight of arrows on the earl of Oxford's vanguard. Notwithstanding their ferocious attack, Oxford was more than a match for his doughty opponent. He had earlier given orders to his archers and men-at-arms to shorten their line and not to move more than ten paces from the banners. Oxford, by his able tactics, succeeded in repulsing Norfolk's attack.

It was against all the odds that Henry, with his much inferior army in numbers, was to gain the victory at Bosworth. Henry, however, always regarded his victory and his elevation to the throne, as an act of divine intervention.

It was a deadly blow for Richard III when his loyal friend, the duke of Norfolk, was killed in hand-to-hand fighting, probably by a stray arrow.

When Richard ordered the earl of Northumberland to place his 3,000 retainers and troops between the Stanleys and the Lancastrian army, he refused to move. According to Polydore Vergil, he remained an idle spectator of the battle while the author of the *Chronicle of Croyland* wrote: 'In the part where the Earl of Northumberland was posted, with a large and well-provided body of troops, there was no opposition made, as not a blow was given or received during the battle.'

Both Richard and Henry now faced enormous problems. Henry feared that although his vanguard was fighting with skill and courage, they would gradually be defeated by superior numbers. They could not afford to continue with the high casualty rate they were enduring.

Henry's next move was to ride forth with the host of cavalry he commanded in reserve across Richard's front intending to make a desperate appeal to Sir William Stanley and his men to join the battle. No sooner did King Richard see his rival riding below Ambion Hill than he made a quick calculation. Seated on his white charger and attended by the knights, squires and yeomen of his household, he made a furious charge on Henry's attendant, brandishing his lance and killing many, who stood in his way. With one blow he killed William Brandon,[15] Henry's standard-bearer, who had shared his master's exile in Brittany. His father, the elder Sir William, was in sanctuary, a victim of Richard's tyranny. Sir John Cheney, a man of powerful physical strength, was flung from the saddle of his horse. Richard was near his hated enemy and actually engaged in combat with him. Henry Tudor was in desperate physical danger, but he fought with a cool courage and skill at Bosworth. He parried Richard's attack.

If Sir William Stanley had not intervened at this stage, together with his 4,000 retainers, the victory would have gone to Richard and the Stanleys would have met a grim fate as traitors. Sir William Stanley, surveying the scene from his vantage point at Hanging Hill near the hamlet of Nether Coton, no longer hesitated. At a signal of his brother Thomas, William galloped with his men to attack Richard's cavalry with the cry 'A Stanley. A Stanley'. Both the brothers were opportunists and wanted to be on the winning side.[16]

Richard on his white charger was unhorsed as his horse sank in the mire. His followers urged him to flee the field, but Richard said that he would die King of England. There are supreme moments in the lives of men and a grandeur nobody can deny them. Crying ever more defiantly 'Treason, treason', Richard was pierced with hideous wounds. He died. Jean Molinet in his *Chroniques* says he was killed by a Welsh soldier at a spot named Sandeford. Meanwhile, seeing the battle was lost, his followers fled, madly pursued, to the villages of Dadlington and Stoke Golding. It had lasted just over two hours.

The shouts of the soldiers crying 'God save King Henry! God save King Henry!' must have been sweet balm to the Tudor after such long years of frustration. There is a tradition that the gold diadem had fallen from Richard's helmet during the battle. Polydore Vergil states that it was Lord Stanley, Henry's stepfather, who placed the royal diadem on his head. He was aged 28, and Henry had mounted a little hill, today known as Crown Hill.

After the battle Henry sent out a circular letter almost immediately, but it contains inaccuracies as to the names of the people killed:

> Henry, by the grace of God, King of England and France, Prince of Wales and Lord of Ireland, strictly chargeth and commandeth upon pain of death, that no man rob or despoil no manner of Commons coming from the field, but suffer them to pass home to their countries and dwelling places with their horses and harness ... and moreover the King ascertaineth you, that Richard Duke of Gloucester, lately called King Richard, was lately slain at a place near Sandeford, within the Shire of Leicester, and there was laid openly that every man might see and look upon him. And also there was slain upon the same field John, late Duke of Norfolk, Thomas, late Earl of Surrey (his son), John late Earl of Lincoln, Francis Viscount Lovel, Sir Walter Deveres, Robert Bracherly and many other knights, squires and gentlemen: on whose souls God have mercy.

Henry does not mention Richard's standard bearer Sir Percival Thriball whose legs were both hewn off.

Several persons named were not killed: the earl of Lincoln, Richard's nephew and heir presumptive was to rebel against Henry VII and to die at the Battle of Stoke; Thomas earl of Surrey was to survive his father many years, taken prisoner along with the earl of Northumberland; Francis Lord Lovel escaped to give Henry plenty of trouble, while William Catesby, who had once betrayed Lord Hastings and been one of Richard III's chief advisers, was taken to Leicester and executed 'as a last reward for his excellent offices' according to the author of *The Continuation of the Chronicle of Croyland.*

The earl of Northumberland only remained a prisoner briefly, making his peace with Henry. After the battle, a Spanish diplomat Diego de Valera wrote a curious account of the demise of Richard III and the establishment of Henry VII as King of England to his sovereigns Ferdinand of Aragon and Isabella of Castile. He ascribed a key role, surely an exaggerated one, before and after Bosworth to the Lord of Tamorland (probably Northumberland), one of the greatest Lords of England. He implies that the Lord of Tamorland's plot was to marry one of his daughters to the dead George of Clarence's son, Edward earl of Warwick, although Richard had declared Clarence illegitimate. Warwick was now the Yorkist heir to the throne of England. It tallies with what we know of Northumberland's enigmatic character, his secrecy and ambition as a Percy. Henry's spies may have brought him word of Tamorland's real intentions.

One of Henry's first acts was to bring back Warwick, a boy of ten, from Sheriff Hutton in Yorkshire, to be consigned to the Tower for the rest of his life. As for Northumberland, after paying homage to Henry and vowing perpetual fidelity, he was released. Henry also sent a valued friend Sir Robert Willoughby to Sheriff Hutton with the express order to escort the Princess Elizabeth of York to London. She had remained in Yorkshire in a state of great uncertainty.

Shakespeare puts into Henry VII's mouth after Bosworth the pregnant words: 'England hath long been mad and scarr'd herself.' Bosworth was one of the most important decisive battles, for it brought to power a ruling dynasty, the Tudors, destined to last one hundred and eighteen years.

V   HENRY VII ATTAINS HIS AMBITION

When he became king in 1485, Henry had little experience; yet with his quick brain, he gradually mastered the duties of a sovereign. A lesser man might well have been deposed by the many Pretenders, who rebelled against him. It is indeed a major historical enigma how this obscure man, familiar with Brittany and parts of France, was able to tackle the immense problems confronting him with such success.[1] Henry was a very clever man, one of the most able ever to reign in England. Even in exile he had trained himself and taken advantage of long discussions with advisers such as John Morton and Richard Fox concerning the duties of kingship, should he ever attain his ambition.

It was a curious twilight age, still largely medieval, but men were already groping for the new age of enlightenment, renaissance, and learning about to ensue. Henry, too, was both medieval in character and outlook and sympathetic to the new age about to dawn. He was to reign without interruption for almost twenty-four years.

One thing he had learnt in exile in Brittany had been the necessity for care in money matters. The king had been too often a begging guest, dependant on borrowing money and not knowing its value. As king, he was to take the greatest possible interest in money, liking to audit his accounts himself. Later he was accused not without justification of avarice, but he was also capable of spontaneous gestures of giving, too.

After two days in Leicester, Henry started for London where he was received ceremonially by the City Fathers on 26 August at Shoreditch, to the sound of trumpets. His early biographer Bernard André, reciting verses, relates that Henry then made for St. Paul's where three banners were displayed, one showing the arms of St. George, another a red fiery dragon on a white and green sarcenet, and a third a dun cow painted upon 'yelowe Tarterne'. Henry spent a few days at the Palace of the bishop of London where he had a joyful reunion with his mother Lady Margaret Beaufort, who now had all her properties and possessions restored to her with additions.

There was no doubt that Henry was *de facto* king by conquest in battle, but his hereditary right to the throne was weak, though he was the male heir of the House of Lancaster through his mother Lady Margaret

Beaufort. She had agreed to waive her right for her son. When parliament assembled at Westminster on 7 November, sovereignty was confirmed to the king as his due, 'not by one, but many titles: so that we are to believe that he rules most rightfully over the English people and that, not so much by right of blood, as of conquest in victory in warfare'.[2] Parliament also expressed a wish that the king should marry the Lady Elizabeth of York, a marriage already agreed to by Henry's binding promise.

The king never wanted to make it seem that he owed his throne to Elizabeth of York rather than to his own claims. He no more desired to be tied to his wife's apron strings than a future King William III. So, his coronation was planned for Sunday, 30 October and Henry's marriage to Elizabeth did not take place until 18 January 1486. There were in any case important, very delicate matters requiring a delay, for Elizabeth had been stigmatized as a bastard by Richard III's parliament and this had to be nullified by Henry's first parliament.[3] A dispensation was also necessary from Pope Innocent VIII because Henry and his future queen were related within the fourth degree of kinship, both being descended from John of Gaunt.

There was much anxiety and criticism when about 30 people, including the dead Richard himself and those of his supporters who had fought against Henry at Bosworth, were attainted on the grounds, clearly a legal fiction, that Henry was already king during the battle.

Thomas Betanson expressed the sentiments of many people when he wrote to Sir Robert Plumpton in the north 'ther was many gentlemen agaynst it, but it wold not be, for yt was the King's pleasure.'[4] The Croyland Chronicler was even more vehement when he exclaimed: 'Oh God! What security shall our kings have henceforth that in the day of battle they may not be deserted by their subjects'.[5] What would become of loyalty and allegiance if men were aware that by obeying the summons of their ruling king they would be subject to death if he were defeated in battle? Men were naturally perturbed because a general pardon had been issued on 24 September. The king himself was an attainted person, an awkward, embarrassing matter for his advisers, but the Justices of the Exchequer Chamber surmounted it, by declaring that on becoming king, Henry had discharged himself *ipso facto* of his attainder.

Before Henry's coronation, he richly rewarded his friends and supporters, such as his uncle Jasper Tudor, who had given devoted service over many years. On 27 October, Jasper was created duke of Bedford. He was now an old bachelor aged fifty-five, but about the beginning of November he became the husband of Catherine Woodville, a sister of the Dowager Queen and widow of Henry Stafford, duke of Buckingham. It is interesting to relate that Jasper had an illegitimate daughter Helen, and was the grandfather of Stephen Gardiner, created bishop of Winchester during the reign of Henry VIII and was to play an important part in its machinations. Thomas Lord Stanley became earl of Derby, and as the king's stepfather was one of the most important magnates in the kingdom until his death in 1504, being created Constable of England, Chief Steward of the duchy of Lancaster and other offices. He was also rewarded with various manors.

His younger brother Sir William Stanley was for ten years an important personage during the reign of the first Tudor. He became Chamberlain of the Household, a Chamberlain of the Exchequer and eventually Constable of Caernarvon Castle and Chief Justice of North Wales. He was also granted various estates in land.

John de Vere, earl of Oxford, who had given invaluable service to King Henry at Bosworth, was rewarded with high offices, being created Admiral of England, Ireland and Aquitaine, Constable of the Tower of London and Keeper of the Lions and Leopards within the Tower. He had been deprived of his estates by the Yorkists but these were now restored to him. As 'Keeper of the Lions and Leopards', Oxford received wages of 12d. per day and 6d. a day for the care of each of the animals in his charge.[6]

Among those who received minor rewards was Sir Rhys ap Thomas, the Welshman whose hesitation to join Henry Tudor on landing had given him much concern. He was created Chamberlain of South Wales in the counties of Carmarthen and Cardigan, Steward of the Lordship of Builth Wells, and Constable and Steward of the Lordship of Brecon. Henry VII wisely did not forget to honour those who had supported him in exile such as Sir Edward Courtenay, now raised to the peerage as earl of Devon,[7] or Christopher Urswick, who became the king's almoner. Even William Stoughton, who had served Henry VI in his youth, was made an alms-knight of St. George's Chapel, Windsor.

As might be expected, Henry soon summoned home from Flanders the exiled bishop of Ely, John Morton, to be rewarded by high office. After the Great Seal was given him, Morton was appointed Chancellor on 6 March 1486 and on the death of his old patron Thomas Bourchier, he was to succeed him as archbishop of Canterbury seven months later. Morton was one of the few people Henry entirely trusted.

Another member of a princely house, Edward Stafford, aged seven, was now restored to the dukedom of Buckingham. He was the son of Catherine Woodville, born at Brecon Castle, and of Henry, who had rebelled against Richard III. Edward Stafford was to adorn the court of Henry VII, a magnificent personality taking a leading part in the jousts, revels and 'disguisings', but his ambition was to lead to his undoing during the early reign of Henry VIII. None of the Staffords died in their beds. The House of Commons chose as their speaker Thomas Lovell, a man well known to Henry VII for he had shared his exile in Brittany.

The king is celebrated for the formation of a royal bodyguard, the so-called yeomen of the king's guard, consisting of a band of fifty tall personable men, later increased.[8] A contemporary work relates that the foundation occurred during 1486, but it was probably founded earlier during the coronation or even after his arrival in London. A curious account is given of yeomen of the guard playing an important part at the marriage of Arthur Prince of Wales. It is in a manuscript in the College of Arms where they are described as 'chosen persones of the hole contreth; proved archers, strong, valiant and bold men; with bright hawberts[?] in their hands, in clothing of large jacketts, whight and grene...' This bodyguard, increased by Henry, became an appanage of English monarchy and the nucleus of the standing army.

The king was preparing for his coronation when London had a devastating attack of the dreaded 'sweating sickness'. It was highly contagious, killing 30,000 people, including two Lord Mayors and six aldermen. While the infection was at its height during October, Henry departed for his manor at Guildford. Fortunately, it was over by 30 October, the day of the coronation. Three days earlier Henry dined at Lambeth Palace with Thomas Bourchier, archbishop of Canterbury for thirty years, who was about to crown him, having performed a similar office at the coronations of Edward IV and Richard III.

For the coronation, massive preparations were made by Sir Reginald (Raynold) Bray and others. Vast purchases were made of silks, satins, of velvet tawny, and cloth of gold. Eleven yards of velvet tawny were needed to buy a long gown for the king.[9] For instance, Richard Joskyne, a tailor and citizen of London mentions: 'My moost dredde (dreaded) soveraigne Henry the VIJ oweth unto me for parcelles delivered unto John Englissh, servaunt the VIth daie of September for 1J (two yards) ... for a gowne for maister Mathewe, sewer to the King's grace.' The bill for various materials bought for the king by Sir Raynold Bray amounted to £358 1s. 11d.

A long-standing tradition and custom ensured that the king should spend the night before his coronation at the Tower, where seven new knights of the Bath were created, including Sir Reginald Bray. From there he rode a charger, a resplendent figure, clad in a 'longe gowne of purpure velvet, furred with ermyns, ... laced with gold and with taselles of Venys gold, with a riche sarpe and garter.' The scene in Westminster Abbey was splendid and colourful. His sword was borne by the newly created earl of Derby, his crown by his uncle Jasper, now duke of Bedford, and his spurs by the earl of Essex. For John de Vere, earl of Oxford, was reserved the distinguished part of bearing the king's train. Archbishop Bourchier performed only the anointing and the crowning, leaving the other rites to John Morton, bishop of Ely, bishops Peter Courtenay of Exeter, John Shirwood of Durham, and Robert Stillington of Bath and Wells. During most of the ceremony the king's mother, Lady Margaret Beaufort, 'wept marvellously', whether for relief and joy or secret fear of the future we do not know.

At the coronation banquet traditional rites were performed: Sir Robert Dymoke, the hereditary King's champion on horseback challenging all-comers, and Jasper Tudor as Steward riding up and down, his horse trapped with cloth of gold.

During the reign of the first Tudor king, Great Councils[11] held at various times were of more importance than the seven parliaments that took place. However, what has been described as the Great Council of 1485 was in reality the parliament. It was the House of Commons with its mouthpiece the Speaker, Thomas Lovell, who beseeched King Henry to marry the Princess Elizabeth of York, a request, which Henry was only too ready to comply with once he had been crowned. We do not possess details of Henry's meetings with Elizabeth before their marriage, but he must have got to know her. Their union was to make his rule more stable, but it must be emphasized that England was in a very lawless, unhappy state at the commencement of the Tudor Age. Many years of strife and rebellions by Pretenders would worry Henry VII until he was accepted by the people. Yet the union of the red and white roses was greatly welcomed. Henry may have been jealous of Elizabeth of York's popularity among the people of England in the very early days of the marriage.

There is a contemporary book[12] written possibly by the Secretary of Francesco Capello, the earliest Venetian ambassador to England on record, which provides very interesting impressions of the writer concerning the English:

> The English are great lovers of themselves, and of everything belonging to them; they think that there are no other men than themselves, and no other world but England; and whenever they see a handsome foreigner, they say that 'he looks like an Englishman', and that 'it is a great pity that he should not be an Englishman', and when they partake of any delicacy with a foreigner, they ask him whether such a thing is made in *their* country ... They have an antipathy to foreigners, and imagine that they never come into their island, but to make themselves master of it, and to usurp their goods, ..

Henry VII was very untypical of the English being partly Welsh by birth and possessing French strains in his blood besides English. As he passed many years in exile, he was far from insular in his outlook and indeed liked and admired foreigners, and later employed them in his service. It helped him to understand the Europe of his age and to become an extremely able diplomatist.

The marriage of Henry with Elizabeth of York was a political one, but it was to develop into a marriage of deep mutual affection. It took place on 18 January 1486 when she was aged not quite twenty-one. She was a beautiful, resplendent bride, attired in her white cloth of gold wedding dressing with gold netting and pearls in her ears.[13] Her father had been very popular, especially among the people of London, and she was to be loved, too. Already cries of 'Elizabeth! Elizabeth!' were raised that winter day as she rode with Henry. It was high time that the wedding should take place, though the papal bulls containing the full dispensation from Pope Innocent VIII did not arrive until June.

Francis Bacon's scholarly and delightful study of *Henry VII*, written to please Henry's direct descendant James I and published in 1622, is not considered today a primary authority. It contains several inaccuracies. He maintains, for instance, that Henry was an indifferent husband and that 'towards his Queen he was nothing uxorious'. It was certainly never a great romance, nor was Henry demonstrative, a man who easily showed his feelings, but husband and wife became attached to one another. We hear of no instance where Henry was unfaithful to her, and in the Tudor age fidelity in marriage was not expected from a king. Both Henry's contemporaries Ferdinand of Aragon and James IV of Scotland married to Henry's elder daughter Margaret had adulterous relationships. His marriage to Elizabeth of York was a happy one and they were in the habit of giving each other small presents.

With all his praise of Henry 'as a wonder for wise men', as 'Solomon', Bacon gives a rather grim, saturnine picture of the first Tudor king. 'For his pleasures,' he wrote, 'there is no news of them.' This gives a false impression because Henry had plenty of interests and pleasures. He was as fond of the chase as the Yorkist kings, loved pageantry and ceremonial and as a Welshman was deeply musical, always insisting that his minstrels, harpists and trumpeters should accompany him on his journeys. A study of his expenditure gives us much information.

During spring (1486) Henry, very uneasy at the depth of feeling still existing in parts of Yorkshire for the Yorkist cause, went on a progress of the eastern counties, travelling to Lincoln and parts of Yorkshire to show himself to his subjects. Elizabeth was with child and remained at Greenwich, a favourite palace. In the course of his progress, Henry learnt that Francis Lord Lovel, who had fought for Richard III at Bosworth, and Humphrey Stafford and his brother Thomas had escaped from sanctuary in Colchester Abbey, and were preparing a rebellion.[14] According to Sir Hugh Conway's testimony many years later, the king was reluctant to credit the conspirators with any such schemes, but 'he was a dark Prince and infinitely suspicious and his time was full of secret conspiracies'.[15]

The Stafford brothers prepared to attack Worcester in the west country while Lord Lovel planned to seize York. The king acted with his customary decisiveness when reaching Pontefract, ordering Uncle Jasper, now duke of Bedford, aged fifty-six but still vigorous as a soldier, to raise 3,000 troops. Meanwhile, he stipulated that all rebels who submitted immediately would be pardoned. This led to the desertion of Lovel's supporters, and the collapse of the Stafford's Worcestershire conspiracy. Humphrey fled to sanctuary in a church at Culham on 11 May, but two days later he was forcibly arrested by the king's officers. Humphrey pleaded that they had no authority to remove him from sanctuary, a matter discussed and argued about by judges. Henry took a great interest in this case, and Hussey, Chief Justice of the King's Bench, asked him not to press for a judicial opinion until the Justices had decided. Eventually, they all agreed that the claim for sanctuary in cases of treason could not be upheld when based on presumptive right alone. So, Humphrey Stafford suffered the death penalty. Henry's policy in such cases was stern repressive measures, generous offers of pardon and ruthless treatment for ringleaders of rebellions. On 2 May, there was a riotous attempt to depose the king in London, but this was equally abortive. These unsuccessful rebellions were to be followed by much more serious affairs. After three months' absence, Henry rejoined Elizabeth in London; they lived much at Sheen, a beautiful palace.

No doubt, the king hoped that his queen would give birth to a son, and in Brittany he had decided that he must be called Arthur to commemorate the king of that name from whom Henry claimed that he traced his lineage. He and his mother constantly at court talked the matter over and because Winchester was the legendary home of Arthur, determined that the queen's child should be born there where Saxon kings had once been crowned. Elizabeth's baby was born to her prematurely eight months after the wedding on 20 September 1486 and the infant prince was healthy and of fair complexion. There were great rejoicings by the people, bonfires were alight in the streets and fountains flowed with wine. Grand preparations for the christening went ahead in Winchester Cathedral. John de Vere, earl of Oxford, was taken by surprise on account of the suddenness of the birth, for he was to act as one of the godfathers. The earl of Derby and Lord Maltravers deputized for him, accompanying the Dowager Queen Elizabeth Woodville to the font where the infant prince was christened Arthur. When Oxford arrived in the cathedral later, he took the baby in his arms, to be confirmed by the bishop of Exeter.[16]

Lady Cecily, Queen Elizabeth's younger sister, took a prominent part in the christening ceremony, carrying the baby prince in her arms. His dress was of crimson cloth of gold, furred with ermine.

Elizabeth was to give her husband many children besides Arthur, but several died in infancy. Their surviving son Edmund named after Henry's father, born in February 1499, was to die little more than a year afterwards. Margaret, Elizabeth and Henry's elder daughter, born during November 1489, was to marry firstly James IV of Scotland and live until 1541, while Henry their second son, born on 28 June 1491, was to eventually succeed his father in 1509. Mary, their younger daughter born during March 1496, was to marry the elderly Louis XII of France and on his death, she wedded the bovine Charles Brandon, duke of Suffolk, son of Henry's standard-bearer killed at Bosworth, which was a love match.

The king's mother, Lady Margaret Beaufort, had been responsible for the infant Arthur's rich mantle of crimson cloth of gold lined throughout with ermine. Although Henry never liked his mother-in-law, the Dowager Queen Elizabeth Woodville, she was one of the godmothers, and the earl of Derby's gift, as one of the godfathers was 'a riche salte of golde, borne by Sir Reginald Bray'. Margaret, with her gift for organization, took immense care in making all the arrangements in the royal nurseries and stipulated that the nursery attendants should be chosen with the greatest diligence and sworn in by the Chamberlain. There were minute regulations for making the king's bed. One of the newly established yeomen of the guard was instructed to 'lepp upon the bedd and roll hym upe and downe', while the queen's bed was made by 'gentill women as the King's bedd is made with men'. It may well be that early in her marriage Queen Elizabeth of York resented a little her mother-in-law's closeness and possessiveness to her husband, though natural enough. A Spanish diplomat, Pedro de Ayala, later emphasizes that Henry's mother had much influence on him and that 'the Queen did not like it,' and another Spanish diplomat alleges that the queen was kept in subjection by her mother-in-law, but this is unlikely to be true. Later the young queen became attached to the Lady Margaret. She and her husband, Lord Stanley, spent the Christmas of 1486 with Henry and Elizabeth at Greenwich Palace before they moved to Sheen.

By November 1486 rumours of a new Yorkist plot against King Henry became widespread, but whether Henry was aware of this until early 1487 is hard to determine. Lambert Simnel, the ten-year-old son of an Oxford organ-maker, was taught by a 'subtile' priest named William Symonds, aged twenty-eight, to impersonate the earl of Warwick, although the real earl was well known to be a prisoner in the Tower. There were false rumours, however, that Warwick, the son of George duke of Clarence was either dead or had escaped from the Tower.

It was in February that King Henry summoned a Great Council at Charterhouse, Sheen. The measures taken during that month and early March were designed by him to combat the threat of Yorkist insurrection.

Now Ireland had always supported the House of York as Richard duke of York, father of Edward, George and Richard had ruled Ireland wisely since 1447 for ten years, and was a well-loved lord lieutenant. George of Clarence, his younger son, had been born in Dublin in 1449 and later held the lord lieutenancy as had the earl of Lincoln. After 1485 Lincoln, a nephew of Richard had at first enjoyed Henry VII's favour, but after the Great Council of early 1487 had taken refuge in flight to the Low Countries and joined the Simnel plot, for he probably cherished secret hopes of the crown. The most powerful personality in Ireland was Gerald Fitzgerald eighth earl of Kildare, described by many as the real King of Ireland. Kildare's sympathies were very much with the Yorkists against Henry VII, the Lancastrian king. William Symonds publicly confessed later in convocation that he had taken the boy Lambert Simnel to Ireland and presented him to the people as earl of Warwick where he was greeted very enthusiastically. King Henry, worried by the news from Ireland, immediately ordered the real earl of Warwick to be taken from the Tower, paraded in the streets of London, and on a Sunday brought to St. Paul's during High Mass, where he was allowed to speak to those already familiar with him. Meanwhile, hoping to scotch the conspiracy, the Great Council resolved to offer pardon throughout England to all offenders implicated in it.

It is hardly likely that Henry suspected his mother-in-law Queen Elizabeth Woodville of being involved in this Yorkist plot, but she was known for her indiscreet tongue and may have complained too openly that Henry had delayed too long setting a date for the coronation of her daughter the queen. For some reason or other, she was deprived of her widow's jointure, which was given to his Queen Elizabeth, and she was removed to the convent at Bermondsey on an annual pension.

Henry had powerful enemies. He considered that his principal enemy was Margaret duchess of Burgundy, a great lady and sister of the late Kings Edward IV, Richard III and of George duke of Clarence. He was to write of her six years later in a letter to Sir Gilbert Talbot referring 'to the great malice that the Lady Margaret of Burgundy beareth continually against us, as she showed lately in sending hither a feigned boy (Lambert Simnel) surmising him to have been the son of the Duke of Clarence'. He mentions also the later rebellion of another 'feigned boy' Perkin Warbeck, who was to impersonate Richard duke of York, younger brother of Edward V. He chiefly blamed Margaret of Burgundy for leading astray Maximilian Archduke of Austria, her stepson, to rebel against the Tudor king when in reality he was a partner. Margaret's part in scheming against Henry may have been exaggerated, but she undoubtedly played an important role. All the Lancastrian writers, including Polydore Vergil, Edward Hall and Francis Bacon in a later age, blame Margaret of Burgundy. Vergil wrote that 'she pursued Henry with insatiable hatred and with fiery wrath, never desisted from employing every scheme which might harm him as a representative of the hostile faction'. Hall refers to her as 'this diabolicall duches', 'lyke a dogge revertynge to her olde vomyte...', while Francis Bacon minces no words in stating 'that she had the spirit of a man and the malice of a woman, abounding in treasure by the greatness of her dower and her provident government in working for the overthrow of Henry Tudor'. She bore such a mortal hatred for the House of Lancaster that she could never forgive her niece for marrying Henry and for uniting the House of Lancaster with the House of York.

The Simnel rebellion was a very serious affair for Henry. A professional army of between 1,500 and 2,000 men was enrolled under their captain Martin Schwartz, a highly experienced mercenary soldier, who may have been a Fleming, German or a Dutchman.[17] It was all done under the authority of the Archduke Maximilian, who was a very competent soldier. This force was known as *The landknechts* of Maximilian, and was partly financed by the Duchess Margaret, who lived mostly in a palace in Malines (Mechelen) in the Low Country. It is recorded that the City of Malines in Flanders gave Margaret of Burgundy 750 livres for her *reyse* to England. A *reyse* may be translated as a venture or a journey, and the money was provided from early 1486 to early 1487 for the invasion of England.[18]

With Margaret's financial aid and support, her nephew the earl of Lincoln, Lord Lovel and Martin Schwartz with their army of about 2,000 mercenary soldiers landed in Ireland on 5 May 1487. The Irish lords, impressed by the size of the army not only recognized Lambert Simnel as the rightful king, but decided to crown him as 'King Edward VI' in Christ Church Cathedral in Dublin.

In England, Henry VII was apprised by his well-informed military intelligence that the rebels were likely to land on the East Anglian coast. He moved troops there, spent Easter at Norwich and went on a pilgrimage to Walsingham. Actually, the rebel army landed at Furness on the Lancashire coast on 4 June, reinforced by some ill-equipped Irish troops. Henry, on hearing of the landing, organized his headquarters at Kenilworth, advancing to Newark and near Stoke in the Midlands ready to resist the invading army.

The king was wise to appoint his uncle Jasper duke of Bedford and the earl of Oxford commanders of the royal army and he was joined by large reinforcements under the earl of Devon at Coventry. It is evident that

Lincoln did not obtain the men he was hoping to switch to his army. His motives for joining the rebellion lay probably in his own ambition to be king.

The Battle of Stoke was the last battle in the 'Wars of the Roses' and was indeed a desperate struggle. It lasted three hours, one hour longer than Bosworth. On Saturday, 16 June, the king rose early and heard two masses. Polydore Vergil gave a later account of the battle, otherwise there is little from contemporary sources. Before 9 a.m. he had reached Stoke, a village a mile from the town. The rebel army, consisting of veteran German mercenaries and badly armed Irish troops, fought courageously but during the battle lost most of their leaders. John, earl of Lincoln, Martin Schwartz, Thomas Broughton, Commander of Lancashire levies, and Thomas Fitzgerald, brother of the earl of Kildare, were all killed. Lord Lovel's fate is somewhat mysterious and obscure. He may have been killed or fled the field. Some say he lay concealed in his house at Minster Lovell, Oxfordshire. He was not attainted until 1495.

Young Lambert Simnel and Symonds, his tutor, were both captured. Realizing that he was the tool of others, Henry ordered that Simnel should be given a job as a scullion in the royal kitchens. Later, he was promoted a falconer. Henry's derisive sense of humour is revealed when he gave an audience to Lord Kildare and other Irish lords two years later. He remarked: 'My masters of Ireland, you will crown apes at last.'[19]

Symonds faced life imprisonment. The king was not vindictive, since not many people were executed after the battle, while some were fined. Nor did Henry deal severely with Lord Kildare in Ireland, retaining him as Lord Deputy after he had taken the oath of allegiance, administered by Sir Richard Edgecombe. He used clemency in pardoning the Irish offenders.

On 4 November 1487, Henry VII returned to London to be given a rousing reception. He rode through the city to St. Paul's to offer thanks for his victory. His queen and mother watched from a window of a house near Bishopsgate and they then returned to Greenwich. Five days later, Henry's second parliament assembled, John Morton, the new archbishop of Canterbury and Chancellor, presiding, and John Mordaunt, a lawyer, as Speaker. Twenty-seven people were attainted, including the earl of Lincoln, killed at Stoke; but the Duke of Suffolk, sorely troubled by the death of his son, was expressly excluded from the act. An important provision was for some of the king's councillors to be given statutory powers to deal with various offences likely to undermine law and order.[20] Another was to confirm the granting of Queen Elizabeth Woodville's forfeited lands to the queen. This parliament was dissolved after five weeks.

It was high time for the queen to be crowned and her coronation was renowned for the joyful spirit animating from it and for its splendour. She was crowned on 25 November (St. Katherine's Day). 'The high and mightie the Duke of Bedforde' (Jasper Tudor) was appointed Great Steward of England, while the earl of Oxford was to be Lord Chamberlayne. The best contemporary account describes it thus:[21]

> The Saturday next before the Day of the queenes Coronacion, her grace being in the Towre of London, after Dyner was royally apparelled, having about her a kyrtle of white clothe of golde of Damaske, and a mantell of the same sute furred with Ermyns, fastenid before her breast with a great lace curiously wrought of golde and silke, and riche knoppes of golde, at the Ende tasselled and her fayre yelow Heare hanging down playne behinde her Back, with a call of Pipes over yt. She had a stirklet of golde richely garnished with pretious stones upon her Head; and so apparelled, departed from her Chamber of Estate unto her Lytter, my Ladie Cecyll, her sister, bearing her Trayne ... the same her grace so procedid from the Towre through the Citie of London to Westminster; all the streets where she shoulde passe by, clensed, dressed, and before with clothes of Tapestrie and arras; and some streetes, as Cheepe, hanged with ryche clothe of golde, velvet, and silke; and along the streets, from the Towre to Powles, stode in order all the crafts of London in their Liveries; and also there was a marvellous sight of People, some in Howses, streets, and Wyndoes, to beholde the sight of the Queenes passing through in her royal apparell...

The earl of Derby took a prominent part as Constable of England and the earl of Nottingham as Marshal of England. On this occasion the king created a number of Knights of the Bath, including the son and heir of the earl of Devonshire, the Lord Dudley and Hugh Conway. On Coronation Day the queen was dressed 'in a kirtle and mantell of purple velvet, furred with ermyne, with a lace afore the mantell, in her Heare, and a circlet of golde richly garnished with Perle, and pretious stones'. We are told, however, that so many people clamoured to cut the Bayclothe that Elizabeth trod upon that in the press some were killed. 'The more pitie' reads the account.

It was the queen's day and the king and his lady mother were merely spectators, sitting privately on a stage built outside one of the windows of Westminster Hall to watch events at the banquet after the Coronation. It was a wonderful pageant with singing children, dressed like angels, as Elizabeth entered Westminster Abbey to be crowned by Archbishop Morton, who had done so much to aid her marriage to Henry and to prepare him for kingship. The first Tudor king was very fortunate in his union with Elizabeth of York.

VI   HENRY'S DIPLOMATIC PROWESS

From the beginning of his reign, Henry was always diplomatically active in his pursuit of peace, for it was essential in a kingdom for a long period ravaged by civil war. War was costly and the king preferred peace. On 12 October 1485, he proclaimed a year's truce with the ancient enemy France and in the following January, he extended it for three years till January 1489. With James III of Scotland, Henry enjoyed on the whole peaceful relations, but James keenly interested in the arts, lacked the necessary ability to deal with his turbulent barons or to rule wild Scotland.[1]

After his defeat at the Battle of Sauchieburn (1488) and subsequent murder, James was succeeded by his son James IV, aged fifteen and a few months, a Renaissance prince, determined to rule his wild and rebellious kingdom. James IV was to give Henry plenty of trouble in his support of the Yorkist Pretender Perkin Warbeck.

Early in his reign, Henry made a commercial treaty with Brittany during July 1486, but France governed by Anne of Beaujeu, Charles VIII's sister, was determined to annex the duchy and during 1488, the Tudor king was faced with a dilemma, though his policy was the right one. For many years Brittany had given him shelter, while France had provided cautious help in his successful attempt to become King of England. Henry decided to compromise and sent Christopher Urswick to France and Brittany for that purpose, but the negotiations failed. France and Brittany were plunged in war in which Edward Woodville, Lord Scales, uncle of the queen, took part with a few hundred volunteers. At the Battle of St. Aubin du Cormier, the Breton army with their allies were defeated. On 20 August 1488, the French forced the Bretons and the ailing Francis II to sign the Treaty of Sablé, in which the duke acknowledged that he was a vassal of France, and promised not to marry his daughter Anne without the consent of Charles VIII and to surrender four towns to France. He died in a few weeks. Henry was not yet officially at war with France, for it was not until 2 October 1492 that he sailed from Dover to Calais with a large army of 25,000 foot and 1,600 horse transported by a fleet of Venetian merchantmen. On 18 October, Henry advanced to besiege Boulogne, but the town was very well fortified and its capture would have presented great difficulties. Consequently he was relieved when Charles VIII made overtures for peace, for at that period the King of France was preoccupied with his plans to invade Italy. An English invasion embarrassed Charles, for it would provoke the disconcerted nobles of Brittany.

The Treaty of Étaples signed on 3 November was very advantageous to England, particularly financially, for by the Treaty the King of France promised to pay 725,000 gold crowns, in instalments of 50,000 francs annually. In return, each country agreed not to help the other's enemies or rebels. Henry was no quixotic adventurer, determined on foreign conquest. What weighed with him were financial considerations, but he was much criticized by the English for abandoning the war. They alleged that he had betrayed his people, obtained a parliamentary grant for war and subjected the people to heavy taxation. The king was realistic enough to see that Brittany had lost her independence and would never recover it.

Spain was to become a great imperial power in the sixteenth century, and Henry had the vision to look ahead and negotiate with her, wanting Spain to become an ally. During 1469, Ferdinand of Aragon had married Isabella of Castile, thus effecting a personal union. With the aid of the church, the 'Catholic' monarchs had succeeded in developing a strong centralized policy. Both were able rulers, and Ferdinand was almost as cunning and skilful in diplomacy as the King of England. During the Franco-Breton war, he became an unreliable ally of Henry's, shirking any fighting himself, but anxious to recover the provinces of Cerdagne and Roussillon formerly pledged to France. Above all, Henry wanted to secure his throne and to acquire the respect of the various European powers. To do so, it was vital to suppress the Pretenders, who rebelled against him during his troubled reign. To show himself master of his kingdom was his ultimate achievement. His dynastic ambitions played an important part in Henry's clever diplomacy, for as early as March 1488 he began to negotiate a marriage between his infant son Arthur, created Prince of Wales in 1490, and Catharine, younger daughter of Isabella and Ferdinand. In these protracted negotiations, the controversial Dr. Rodrigo Gonzalez de Puebla, first sent to England as resident Spanish ambassador in 1487 and winning Henry's confidence, played a vital part. In the drafting of the Treaty of Medina signed near Valladolid (27 March 1489) de Puebla was prominent, for the negotiations foreshadowed the later marriage.

Henry's active diplomacy included the renewal of the ancient treaty with Portugal first signed in 1387 during the reign of Richard II and he entrusted Dr. Thomas Savage and another diplomat with a mission to secure the ratification of King John of Portugal, who was also rewarded with the Garter. During January he made a further political and commercial treaty with Denmark.

The powerful Republic of Venice was of significant importance towards the end of the fifteenth century. Henry pursued a policy of profitable trade with that state. Her merchants bought much cloth and wool from England, and in exchange brought to our shores spices from the East, books, glassware, and the heavy sweet wines of the Levant.[2] Wool exported to Venice amounted to 600 sacks per annum, and it had to be carried in English ships. However, King Henry's severe customs against the Venetians exasperated the Republic. He was far-seeing also in his relations with Tuscany, estabishing a Consul at Pisa in 1486. Four years later he negotiated a six years' treaty with Florence, providing free intercourse of trade and an English wool staple at Pisa. When Ludovico Sforza, duke of Milan, feared the might of France, the King of England signed a treaty with him (6 October 1490). Italian diplomats in Henry's later reign marvelled at his knowledge of Italian affairs, but he never interfered in Italy. His relations with the Borgia Pope Alexander VI, who succeeded Innocent VIII in 1492, were benevolent, and Alexander Borgia was to live until 1503. His famous son, the ruthless Cesare, nearly succeeded at the beginning of the sixteenth century in making the Papal States the heart of a limited Italy.

With Maximilian, Emperor of Austria and King of the Romans from 1486, founder of the house of Habsburg and married firstly to Mary of Burgundy, the heiress to Flanders, the Duchess Margaret of Burgundy's stepdaughter, Henry's relations were on the whole hostile. Their characters were completely opposed. While Henry was cautious, tenacious and dependable, Maximilian was volatile, mercurial, obsessed by restless ambition and a perfidious ally.

By his marriage to Mary of Burgundy in 1477, Maximilian annexed her rich lands to the Habsburg Empire. Flanders was a flourishing state, its many waterways leading to the important port of Antwerp, a centre of England's overseas trade. After Mary of Burgundy's[3] death in an accident, Maximilian became even more powerful.

Though Henry preferred diplomacy to warfare, he took considerable trouble to promote archery according to various authorities.[4] Firearms and artillery were to creep into use in his early reign, but the soldiers still mostly depended on the bow. Henry was himself partial to archery and ordered in the year 1498 'all the gardens which had been continued time out of mind without Mooregate of London, to be destroyed and instead to be made a plain field for archers to shoot in'. Both his sons Arthur and Henry were very fond of archery. Indeed, Prince Henry 'shotte as strong and as great a lengthe as any of his garde',[5] and Princess Margaret, Henry's elder daughter, showed skill on her way to Scotland in 1503 to marry James IV in killing a buck with an arrow in Alnwich Park.

Henry VII did not add much to the fleet, which partly descended to him from the Yorkist King Edward IV. Of the four ships which came down to him all disappeared or were reconstructed within a few years. The records show[6] that Henry only added six ships to his fleet. Two of them *The Regent* and *The Sovereign* were large vessels for their day. While exiled, Henry Tudor had seen a French ship that attracted him and *The Regent* was modelled on her, being of 600 tons. This ship was well supplied with guns, possessing 225, most of them serpentines, the largest naval gun in use at that time. They weighed probably about 300 pounds. Like similar warships, *The Regent* carried bows and sheaves of arrows as part of her armament. *The Sovereign* was a little smaller, for she carried only 141 guns. She was built about 1490. Henry is commemorated for constructing at Portsmouth the first drydock ever supplied for the Royal Navy during 1495-1497. It is known that the king added two other new ships to his little fleet. These were The *Sweetstake* and *The Mary Fortune*. To help trade, Henry was wont to hire out his best ships to merchants. The first Tudor king was also responsible for persuading parliament to pass two acts, which may be described in a later age as Navigation Acts.[7] One of 1485, lamenting the decay of English shipping in recent times, decreed that for the future no wines from Guienne or Gascony should be sold in the dominions of the King of England except those carried in English, Irish, or Welsh ships or men of Calais. Another clause enacted that the king's subjects were prohibited from using foreign shipping for export or import trade if sufficient English shipping was available in the port they used. Insular policy, perhaps, but highly necessary in 1485 when England lay so impoverished.

Parliament in January 1489 had voted Henry a large subsidy for the purpose of despatching an expedition to Brittany. The total amount voted was £100,000, but of this only £27,000 seems to have been raised.[8] So, Henry resorted to highly unpopular taxation mainly on personal property and the annual produce of lands. Nowhere was this taxation more keenly resented than in Yorkshire where Richard III had been popular, Durham and parts of Northumberland. Henry Percy, fourth earl of Northumberland had the odious duty as lord-lieutenant of collecting it, though well aware of the popular discontent and the danger that it might flare into rebellion. Northumberland was unpopular in Yorkshire because he had remained inactive at Bosworth. He summoned the malcontents whose leader was John à Chambre to one of his seats, Topcliffe near Thirsk in Yorkshire, where heated exchanges took place between the earl, John à Chambre and his followers. It is probable that Northumberland somewhat sympathized with the objections raised by à Chambre, but his arrogant manner was enough to incense his rebellious opponents. Stung by some coarse and insulting expression of John à Chambre, Northumberland exclaimed furiously: 'Thou art a scurvy knave, and they that hearken to thee hearken to a false and dangerous adviser'. He advised them to depart to their homes and to refrain from treasonable language. It was 28 April 1489, and since Henry Percy had few servants attending him, it was easy for the unruly mob to murder him. He had lacked the magnetism or charisma of Hotspur and was totally incapable of rousing devotion in others.

The death of the equivocal earl was probably regarded with mixed feelings by Henry VII, but the murder of the Warden-General of the East and Middle Marches towards Scotland could not remain unpunished. The leader of the malcontents, John à Chambre, was captured and executed while Sir John Egremont escaped to the court of the Duchess Margaret of Burgundy.

The principal object the king had in mind throughout his reign was to curb the power of the great feudal barons.[9] The prevailing custom of maintaining large bodies of retainers on their properties and estates was extremely repugnant to him. Even those who had given Henry most devoted service were not spared. Francis Bacon relates the celebrated story, not supported by documents, how on one occasion the king was being entertained at Castle Hedingham in Essex by John de Vere, earl of Oxford, who employed a multitude of retainers. On taking leave of his host, Henry thanked Oxford for his lavish hospitality, but fined him for offending against the maintenance laws, saying: 'By my faith, my lord, I thank you for my good cheer, but I may not endure to have my laws broken in my sight.' One might think that Henry should have made an exception in Oxford's case. However, there was no question of litigation. We are merely told that the earl *compounded* for his offence[10] for no less than 15,000 marks.

It is evident that the abuse of the laws continued during the reign of the first Tudor king and attempts were made to remedy matters. Parliament enacted in 1487 that the good rule of the realm was being subverted by unlawful maintenance and the giving of liveries. To remedy this, the great offices of state were authorized to summon and pardon offenders. A more effective law was passed in 1504 stating that liveries and retainers were still being given and received. Consequently, it was provided that penalties of £5 per month for each man who was retained were authorized for breaches of the Act. The 1504 Act still allowed the retaining of household servants. Earlier during 1485-6 Chief Justice Hussey had referred cynically to lords who swore oaths not to retain and then did so.[11]

Henry's policy in wishing to curb the practice of livery and maintenance was to make clear to his subjects that their first allegiance must be owing to him, their king. He stressed that their duties to him must take precedence over lesser duties to a tenant-in-chief. There was no standing army in those times, and when Henry rarely declared war he pursued the custom of making 'indentures of war' with his lords, who then enlisted their own retainers. Henry succeeded in controlling the system rather than abolishing it. Indeed, he may not have wanted to, for it had a useful function to fulfil in finding a way to raise an army.

There were several cases where noblemen offended against the existing laws. For instance in 1494, the earl of Devon bound himself by recognizance not to employ retainers contrary to the law. Two years later, however, he made two payments in part discharge of the recognizance because he had been found guilty of a breach of the bond. Again in 1506 the young earl of Derby (Henry's stepfather, died in 1504) bound himself to pay £1,000 in six instalments in part payment of a fine incurred by an uncle for unlawful retaining under the 1504 law. Sometimes cases were decided by the Justices of the Peace or taken against offenders in the Star Chamber. Others appeared before the Council. The most important case concerned George Neville Lord Burgavenny (Abergavenny), a nobleman implicated in the Cornish rebellion in 1497. Burgavenny incurred a huge fine of £70,650 for retaining 471 men for thirty months between June 1504 and December 1506. He was compelled to enter into recognizances for the payment of the fine. Later it was reduced to £5,000, payable in ten annual instalments because Henry was more interested in obtaining the available money than with enforcing the full rigour of the law. Burgavenny, however, later received a royal pardon from Henry's successor and served as Chief Captain of the Royal Army (1514).[12]

Henry showed moderation in creating new peers, yet he was eager for them to attend his court and suspicious of those who stayed away from it. Two thirds of the peers attended his Councils. His court was far more luxurious and splendid than is often alleged since Henry loved pageantry, and his tournaments, pomps, and progresses were designed to impress foreign courts with the stability of his rule. He was only too conscious, however, of its instability owing to the impersonations of Pretenders. Where display and magnificence were necessary, such as the marriages of Arthur Prince of Wales and of Margaret Tudor, he spared no expense. He was certainly not niggardly. He could be hard and grasping in the administration after eighteen years' rule of escheated or forfeited estates, and he acquired a further revenue of £6,264 from wardships, but to gain a land revenue of some £42,000 towards the end of his reign shows his financial acumen and must be praised rather than criticized.

VII   PERKIN WARBECK

Much the most serious Yorkist plot against Henry VII was that of Perkin Warbeck lasting six years. It deeply troubled the king. According to the Pretender's later confession, he was the son of John Warbeck or Osbeck, a boatman and collector of customs in Tournay in Flanders and his mother's name was Katharine de Faro.[1] He was born in 1474 or 1475. His first employer was a man named Berlo. According to Perkin Warbeck's confession, Berlo:

> set me with a merchant at Middleborough to learn the language (presumably English) with whom I dwelled from Christmas unto Easter; and then I went into Portyngale (Portugal) in the company of Sir Edward Brampton's wif in a ship which was called the Quene's ship ...

Warbeck does not specifically mention Sir Edward Brampton, but he must have travelled on this ship, for no lady in that early Tudor age would have been allowed to embark on her own.

Sir Edward was Jewish by birth, born in Lisbon and formerly very familiar with Edward IV's court. Edward had been his godfather, and 'laved him in the sacred font'. He was Brampton's patron and Brampton had served the king with some diligence. Whilst on the ship Brampton entertained young Warbeck with his account of the Yorkist court and he listening eagerly, lapped up every word. When during 1489 an embassy from Henry VII had arrived in Lisbon, Sir Edward Brampton had done his utmost to make himself agreeable entertaining them at his home. Whilst in Lisbon during his strange wandering early life, Perkin Warbeck served for one year a knight called Vacz de Cogna, who only 'had one eye'.[2]

Afterwards the adventurer entered the service of a Breton merchant named Pregent Meno, who eventually brought him to Ireland during the autumn of 1491. There the gullible citizens of Cork, deeply impressed because Warbeck was both handsome and affable, particularly when dressed in the silk clothes of his master, paid homage to him. At first they declared that he was son of the duke of Clarence, who had been born in

Ireland, but he refused to acknowledge it; then they set him up as a bastard of Richard III, which he also denied. At last they insisted that he was Richard duke of York, younger brother of Edward V, one of the princes in the Tower about whose fate nobody could be certain, though he had disappeared together with his brother during the late summer of 1483. No evidence exists that Perkin denied being 'Richard'. According to his own story, he merely said 'and so, against my will, they made me to learn English, and taught me what I should do and say'. Both the earl of Desmond within whose domain the town of Cork lay and the earl of Kildare at first encouraged his pretensions. Desmond corresponded with James IV of Scotland on the subject, on 2 March 1492. It is evident that Perkin Warbeck remained in Ireland during the winter and that after 3 October 1491 Perkin appeared before the Mayor of Cork, John Le Wellen to swear that he was not the son of the duke of Clarence (the earl of Warwick, Clarence's real son was still Henry's prisoner in the Tower).

On leaving Ireland, Warbeck was invited to France by Charles VIII, who wanted to embarrass King Henry and weaken his power if matters spread to a war. Charles VIII was now married to a daughter of the Duke Francis of Brittany, now dead. To carry his invitation, Charles sent two French envoys: Loyte Lucas and a former French Secretary of Henry's named Frion, now in the service of the King of France. Whilst there, Warbeck was treated with great honour by Charles, who gave him a guard commanded by the Sieur de Concressault. He was now joined by a number of disaffected Yorkists, including Sir George Neville. However, one of the clauses of the Treaty of Étaples (3 November 1492) stipulated that Charles VIII would not aid any of Henry VII's rebels, so he was compelled to dismiss Perkin from his kingdom.

The adventurer then continued his journey to the Low Countries where he was received with joy by the Duchess Margaret of Burgundy. It seems probable that Margaret really believed that the impostor Warbeck was her nephew. She had only seen the real Richard duke of York once in her life when she visited England in 1480. Her nephew born in 1473 would have been scarcely seven. Otherwise Margaret had been overseas for 25 years. It is difficult to believe that she considered him a fraud when she made such efforts on his behalf.[3] Both Polydore Vergil and Edward Hall shared the belief that Margaret was convinced that her long lost nephew had been found. Polydore Vergil wrote that Margaret received Perkin (Peter) '... as though he had been revived from the dead ... so great was her happiness that the pleasure seemed to have disturbed the balance of her mind'. Hall minces no words alleging that Margaret thought 'to have gotten God by the foote when she had the Devill by the Tail'. Molinet, the French chronicler, named Perkin Warbeck as 'Pierrequin

Wezebecque'. The Dutch word 'weze' means 'orphan'. There were many Yorkist exiles at Margaret's court and they made much of Perkin. The only known portrait of the Pretender to have survived is one of him in the museum at Arras. It shows a curiously aristocratic young man with long hair and a slight irregularity about his eyes. A Venetian ambassador wrote in 1497 that he was not handsome, indeed his left eye rather lacks lustre but he is intelligent and well spoken.[4]

Known in her own day as a munificent patron of the arts under whose patronage the first book printed in English was published by William Caxton at Bruges, Margaret of Burgundy harboured a grudge against Henry VII. She disliked him not only for depriving the Yorkist dynasty of their throne, but for depriving her of a portion of her income. Whilst they were alive Margaret had benefitted from various trading licences granted by her brothers Edward IV and Richard III, but these were not renewed under the first Tudor king. She certainly resented these losses. Her energetic actions on behalf of her supposed nephew may have been partly motivated by this loss of income.

Both Margaret and Perkin wrote to Isabella of Castile imploring her to succour 'this last sprig of her family'. However, neither Isabella nor Ferdinand ever believed that Warbeck was genuine.[5] They were too shrewd, writing to de Puebla, their ambassador in England, 'as for the affair of him who calls himself the duke of York we hold it for a jest'. Perkin's letter was far from convincing, stating that he was nearly nine years when he had escaped from the Tower with the connivance of the lord, who had come to murder him, when the real Richard duke of York was aged ten. Perkin's account of how he was smuggled abroad was so vague that it cannot have deceived Ferdinand or Isabella. Margaret in her letter to Isabella of Spain claimed that she had been able to recognize 'Richard' (Warbeck), and had miraculously preserved him from death.

Henry VII, with his sure political instinct, realized very soon that the Pretender presented a grave danger to his dynasty, for Perkin was recognized by several European powers: the Duchess Margaret, the King of Denmark, James IV of Scotland and the Emperor Maximilian and his Archduke. Furthermore, his dearest wish to conclude a marriage between his son and heir Prince Arthur and Princess Catherine of Aragon, Isabella's younger daughter, would be hampered or even ruined while a Pretender threatened his dynastic hopes. By July 1493 Henry possessed much knowledge about the Pretender's background, and knew that his father was a boatman and that he was a native of Tournay in Flanders.

Perkin while staying at the Duchess Margaret's court was astute enough to promise her that when he became king he would restore her trading licences and repay the debt still owed to her on her dowry. It was also proposed that the lady should receive the manor of Hunsdon and the castle and town of Scarborough in England. One suspects that this was part of a secret deal between Margaret and Sir William Stanley.

Stanley, the younger brother of Henry's stepfather, was his Chamberlain, a man of great wealth. It came as no surprise to the king that Stanley had stooped to treason, for he had suspected this for some time. Stanley was friendly with Sir Robert Clifford[6] and his special act of treason was to send abroad Clifford for the purpose of communicating with Warbeck. The date of Clifford's understanding with Sir William to travel to Flanders was 18 March 1493. This happened just after Perkin had been driven out of France and was an honoured guest of the Duchess Margaret in Malines. It is likely that Stanley with his wealth wished to insure himself against the risk that the Pretender might invade the kingdom, succeed in expelling Henry and reinstate a Yorkist dynasty. As Clifford managed to maintain his favour with Henry VII, it is probable that he was a kind of double agent. It was on his evidence that Stanley was subsequently arrested and tried for treason[7] in Westminster Hall on 30 and 31 January 1495. Although Sir William's intervention at Bosworth had helped Henry Tudor to win the battle it availed him nothing. A number of other persons had also been attainted and executed. Stanley was executed on 16 February 1495. Henry, subject to sudden impulses, paid the cost of his funeral.

From the Emperor Maximilian and his son the Archduke Philip, the Pretender received enormous support. Maximilian, often hostile to Henry, smarted with resentment that the king had made peace with France. He and his son provided Warbeck with an escort of 30 halberdiers dressed in the York livery of mulberry and blue decorated with white roses. Warbeck, who called himself '*King Richard IV*', rode beside Philip with whom he was on very amicable terms on his visits to Louvain and Antwerp during October 1494. English merchants, who happened to be present in Antwerp, were furious at this Yorkist propaganda, particularly when the impostor's arms proclaiming him Prince of Wales were displayed in the house of the English merchant adventurers. Henry, very concerned, had already sent an embassy headed by the able Sir Edward Poynings and William Warham, later archbishop of Canterbury, to Burgundy to remonstrate with Philip that he was harbouring an impostor. On Henry's instructions, they blamed the Lady Margaret duchess of Burgundy for deceiving Philip rather than the Emperor himself. Henry alleged that she was the dupe of another 'feigned lad'.

In Scotland where Warbeck took refuge for two years, he was warmly welcomed by the affable, able James IV and was received at Stirling as 'Prince Richard of England'. In his calculating way, the king wanted to embarrass Henry VII. Special taxes were raised to allow the Pretender an allowance of £1,344 per annum paid monthly. James approved of a marriage between Warbeck and Lady Catherine Gordon, daughter of the second earl of Huntly, but she was only distantly related to James. It is far from likely that the king believed that Warbeck was Richard duke of York. He was well aware that most European rulers had grown cynical about the Pretender's claim. Warbeck was married to Lady Catherine Gordon in Edinburgh about 13 January 1496. His most recent biographer relates that Perkin was dressed in a 'spousing gowne of white damask' and the king took part in the jousting that followed.

There is a love letter from Perkin to Lady Catherine, supposedly written at the end of 1495 revealing that the Pretender had a marked romantic streak:

> All look at your face, so bright and serene that it gives splendour to the cloudy sky; all look at your eyes as brilliant as stars, which make all pain to be forgotten and turn despair into delight. All look at your neck which outshines pearl. All look at your fine forehead, your purple light of youth, your fair hair, at one word, at the splendid perfection of your person. Most noble lady, my soul, look mercifully down about me your slave, who has ever been devoted to you from the first hour he saw you. Love is not an earthly thing, it is heaven born. Do not think it below yourself to obey love's dictates.

What lady could resist such verbal eloquence?

What is certain is that the King of Scotland invested a considerable amount of money in Warbeck's cause and was willing to finance the Pretender's followers, who swarmed about it. At this period James was attracted to a diplomatic marriage with a Princess of Spain or at least to the possibility.[8]

By the end of 1495 Henry found himself menaced by James IV, Margaret of Burgundy and by the Emperor Maximilian. At this juncture, however, he conceived a brilliant idea, leading to a masterly stroke of diplomacy. He proposed to negotiate for a marriage between his elder daughter Margaret and James IV and to employ Bishop Richard Fox, an extremely able negotiator for this purpose. James, however, continued for a while to harbour the Pretender, viewing him as a useful ally in his diplomatic war with England. His attitude was equivocal, for he hoped to come to satisfactory terms with Bishop Fox over the proposed marriage, but if these failed, abide by his agreement with Warbeck to invade England by September 1496 and seize Berwick on the border.

Meanwhile, the European powers vied with one another to find the best way for getting hold of the Pretender. France under Charles VIII, who was at war with Italy, offered the huge sum of 100,000 crowns to James to buy Warbeck, but the King of Scotland refused the offer.

The celebrated Cornish Rebellion during the summer of 1497 was to have a significant influence on Perkin Warbeck's fortunes. To resist the threatened invasion by James IV and Warbeck, Henry summoned a Great Council, which met from 24 October to 5 November 1496. During its deliberations it was agreed that parliament, when it assembled in January, would grant £120,000, and the king immediately sought to raise loans on the security of its pledge.[9] The direct taxation proposed in parliament was extremely unpopular in the country, especially in Cornwall where the Cornish blamed the king's counsellors rather than Henry himself. Although according to later traditions Henry had enjoyed much support in Cornwall, for many had suffered for his cause as fellow exiles in Brittany, some were now much discontented with his rule, holding serious grievances. Moreover, since his accession, Henry had done little to help the country's inhabitants, although he had seemed to lavish favours on the Cornish gentry. Matters came to a head when the tin-miners refused to accept some regulations set by King Henry whereby they lost the ancient privileges protecting their livelihood.[10]

The leaders of the rebellion were men of different backgrounds: a Bodmin blacksmith, Michael Joseph, and Thomas Flamank, a lawyer. In May 1497 they persuaded 3,000-6,000 Cornishmen in St. Keverne to march across the Tamar to eventual defeat at Blackheath. In Wells the Cornishmen were joined by James Touchet, seventh Baron Audley, whose family had been devoted Lancastrians, but may have held grievances of being insufficiently rewarded. Henry, with his customary foresight, took massive steps to defend London, ordering the loyal and devoted Lord Daubeny to station himself south with a force of 8,000 or more men. The rebels had no success when they marched for Kent where Wat Tyler and Jack Cade had once defied the monarchy. Henry himself lay at his headquarters at Lambeth with an army of 25,000 men, having sent his queen and Prince Henry, aged six, to the palace in the Tower. His forces outnumbered the insurgents. In the ensuing battle the royal army triumphed, though suffering a loss of 300 men killed. The opposing rebels were defeated, many being slain and its leaders captured. London supported the king, giving him a splendid reception as he rode over London Bridge. In his many encounters with his foes Henry always revealed his religious faith. After knighting the mayor and two of his officers, Henry rode on to old St. Paul's to return thanks to God for his victory. He then joined Queen Elizabeth in the Tower. He was not vindictive for only Flamank, Joseph and Lord Audley suffered the death penalty. Flamank and Joseph were taken from the Tower to be hanged at Tyburn, while Audley was beheaded on Tower Hill. As was his custom, the other captured rebels were fined. The king's troubles were far from over, for Perkin Warbeck was now to invade the West Country.

When we consider Perkin Warbeck as a man, it is incredible that he duped so many people. Bacon writes, however, in his *History of the Reign of Henry VII*[11] that the Pretender 'had such a crafty and bewitching fashion both to move pity and to induce belief as was like a kind of fascination and enchantment'.

Only a few days after quelling the Cornish insurrection on 5 July 1497 Henry instructed Bishop Fox to demand the surrender of Perkin Warbeck from the King of Scotland. Any agreement with an impostor was of no value whatsoever. Henry was anxious to find a way to reopen the negotiations for his daughter to marry James IV, so his attitude was far from unfriendly. Ferdinand and Isabella of Spain, too, favoured the match, wanting to consolidate an alliance against France. Their able ambassador Pedro de Ayala, with the reputation of acquiring the confidence and friendship of those monarchs to whom he was accredited, succeeded in establishing very amicable relations with James.[12] For some time the King of Scotland had wanted to get rid of Perkin.

On 6 July Perkin Warbeck sailed from Ayr in a Flemish ship called *Cuckoo* or *Kekeout* (a Dutch name), taking his beautiful wife Catherine and about thirty followers. She had been given $3^1/_2$ ells of Rouen cloth to make herself a sea-gown. Perkin arrived in Cork on 26 July only to be disapppointed with lack of support. So he continued his journey sailing with a small fleet and about a hundred men to Whitesand Bay near Land's End, where he thought that, owing to hostility to King Henry, many would join him. After sending his wife and her ladies to St. Michael's Mount, Perkin had himself proclaimed King '*Richard IV*' at Bodmin. The Pretender had now been joined by several thousand countrymen. He marched on to Exeter with his reinforcements, prepared to besiege the city, but Perkin lacked artillery and armour, which was absolutely essential if he had any chance of success. Exeter was stoutly defended by Sir Edward Courtenay, earl of Devonshire, although the rebels bravely attacked the north and east gates. Their losses were heavy, for 400 men were killed. Undeterred, they moved to Taunton.

Henry VII wrote to the bishop of Bath and Wells on 20 September 1497:

> that Perkin had been refused entrance to the city of Exeter by the Earl of Devonshire, Sir William Courtenay, Sir Piers Edgecombe and

other noblemen ... but it was so defended (blessed by God)! that Perkin lost above three or four hundred men. (Gairdner mentions 200 men). We have proclaimed also, that who so bringeth the said Perkin alive unto us, shall have the sum of a thousand marks and all their offences forgiven first and last.

At Taunton Warbeck having lost all hope and his courage failing, made his celebrated confession on his imposture already mentioned.

The Pretender's letter to his mother, the former Katharine de Faro, written from Exeter, is important because if genuine, as it very probably was, is absolute proof that the claims of Perkin to be 'Richard Duke of York', Edward IV's younger son, were false.[13]

The king acted decisively. For the purpose of securing the sea ports in case the adventurer attempted to seek refuge abroad, he sent Lord Daubeney, the Lord Chamberlain, with experienced forces to intercept Warbeck. However, on 21 September, the Pretender's nerve cracked, for at midnight he deserted his men, taking 60 followers on horseback. Lord Daubeney's army was at Glastonbury while Henry and the young duke of Buckingham with their forces were hard on the road for Taunton. Perkin himself made for sanctuary at Beaulieu in Hampshire with a few followers. In a desperate state, Perkin implored members of the king's household when they reached Beaulieu to intercede for him with Henry. He would make a full confession if he were granted his life. To the king, then at Taunton, the adventurer made his humiliating confession that his real name was Piers Osbeck or Warbeck of Tournay and that his father had been a boatman. Henry took Warbeck with him to Exeter, from where he sent for the Pretender's wife still at St. Michael's Mount. To her the king behaved with much understanding, commiserating with her that she had been made the victim of a despicable imposture and making his captive repeat his story. He then sent her to his queen, who had just returned from Walsingham. There Catherine's beauty and grace gave her the name of 'The White Rose', according to Francis Bacon, but she deeply suffered from Warbeck's cruel deception. She was to marry three more husbands James Strangeways, Matthew Cradock and Christopher Ashton, and to adorn Queen Elizabeth's court.

After a few of the ringleaders had been executed at Exeter, the collection of fines amounting to £14,699 from those involved in the rebellion gave much satisfaction to King Henry. At first Perkin was treated with clemency by Henry or at least not too severely. The king reached Westminster on 27 November, while Perkin was paraded through the streets as if he was some kind of monster. At Henry's court, keepers were appointed to watch over him, but there was no real restraint on his liberty. On 9 June in the following year

(1498), he managed to escape to the Charterhouse at Sheen. He was subsequently recaptured and placed in the stocks at Westminster where he was forced to repeat his confession. A few days later, he was again placed in the stocks in Cheapside in the morning till three in the afternoon. From there he was brought to the Tower to be more rigorously confined. When conveyed before the Archduke Philip's ambassador, the bishop of Cambray, somebody demanded why he had deceived the Archduke and others. The king informed the bishop of Cambray that Warbeck had deceived the Pope, Charles VIII of France, the Emperor Maximilian, the King of Scotland and almost all the princes of Christendom except Ferdinand and Isabella of Spain. Their ambassador de Puebla was present on this occasion. Warbeck swore on oath that the Duchess Margaret of Burgundy had known that he was not King Edward's son.

Whilst in the Tower, Warbeck seems to have connived with the weak-brained earl of Warwick, still in that fortress, in a plot. On 16 November 1499, he was charged with trying to escape from the Tower by bribing his custodians. A week later, Perkin and his companion John à Water, Mayor of Cork, were hanged at Tyburn.

King Henry can be criticized for his ruthless behaviour to Edward earl of Warwick, a young nobleman, who was evidently half-witted. However, so long as Warwick lived, he threatened Henry's security. He was the foremost Yorkist heir. Brought before John de Vere, earl of Oxford in Westminster Hall, he was found guilty of treason and condemned to death. He was beheaded on Tower Hill aged twenty-four. Did the king need to be so harsh? He was mindful that Ferdinand and Isabella, engaged in the long negotiations preceding the marriage of Catherine of Aragon to the Prince of Wales, his dearest wish, might cease negotiations altogether unless Warwick was dead. There were other Yorkist heirs who were still alive to remain an embarrassment to Henry. Although John, earl of Lincoln, had been killed at the Battle of Stoke, there remained Edmund earl of Suffolk, third son of Elizabeth and John de la Pole, duke of Suffolk, who had fled to Flanders and another brother William.[14]

King Henry's patient diplomacy with James IV of Scotland now bore fruit. Political affairs now favoured him, for Pedro de Ayala, Spanish ambassador to James IV, working for peace between England and Scotland, succeeded in making a truce, which was to last for seven years. It was signed at Ayton in 1497. The scene was now laid for further negotiations for the eventual marriage of Margaret Tudor with James.

It must be stressed that Henry's outlook was curiously medieval, but he was a blend of an early renaissance king with one part of his character clinging to the past. For instance, he liked to employ foreigners at court, though well aware of the English xenophobia for those of different birth.

His favourite astrologer was an Italian Master Parron-Gulielmus Parronus Placentinus as he called himself in his Latin works.[15] He may even have influenced Henry concerning what might be described as 'the Judicial murder of the Earl of Warwick', but he never mentions Warwick by name. 'It is expedient,' he wrote:

> that one man should die for the whole people and the whole nation perish not, for an insurrection cannot occur in any state without the death of a great part of the people, and the destruction of many great families with their property.

Parron and his family came from Piacenza in Italy and were typical of Italians of the Renaissance, who made themselves careers abroad in literature or art. Henry VII was his patron and under his patronage organized a regular astrological forecasting business. He told King Henry that he had a high opinion of printing and that it was one of the great new inventions of the day. Astronomers and many others often deride astrology as far from proven, but it is foolish to dismiss it so, because many astrologers besides the famous Nostradamus have made true predictions, difficult to explain. In the autumn of 1499 when Parron was aged over thirty, he bragged to Henry that the readers of his prognostications for the current year had been forewarned of the abnormally heavy rains that had fallen in England. In his writings Parron discusses the power of the stars, particularly in his work *De Astorum VI Fatali*.[16] Not only Parron, but Italian men of letters were wont to flatter the king immediately after the Battle of Bosworth, simultaneously denouncing Richard III. For instance, Giovanni Gigli praised Henry VII's marriage with Elizabeth of York, and when mentioning the birth of their son Arthur depicted Richard as the murderer of his own nephews.

Parron, however, made at least two entirely untrue predictions in his *Liber de Optimo fato, Henrici Eboraci ducis et optimum ipsius parentum*, composed after 2 April 1502, the date of Prince Arthur's death at Ludlow, and finished before 11 February 1503, when his mother Elizabeth of York died in the palace of the Tower of London at the early age of thirty-seven. Parron had insisted that the Queen would live to over eighty. In lamenting the death of Elizabeth, who was much loved, Sir Thomas More puts into her mouth a complete rejection of astrology, a view held, perhaps, by a majority of courtiers. About this time, Parron felt it advisable to depart from Henry's court and to seek his fortunes elsewhere. Whether or not Henry and Elizabeth had commissioned him, Parron presented to the king and queen a horoscope of their second son Henry in which he made false forecasts. He discusses the success of Prince Henry's future reign and the felicity of his married life, only true for the early part. He predicted a large number of sons, but Henry VIII, as we know, left one legitimate son Edward VI, who survived his father six years.

Another frivolous Pretender claiming, like Lambert Simnel, to be the earl of Warwick, now appeared. His name was Ralph Wilford, a cordwainer's son from Suffolk, and he was carefully coached by an Augustinian friar. Henry VII was tired to death of these impersonations, and he was to visibly age, looking more than forty-two in 1499. England was ravaged by the plague, so Henry decided to send his children into the country while taking his queen to Calais. He hoped that she would recover there from giving birth to another son Prince Edmond and from her many confinements. At Calais, a walled city, Henry and Elizabeth met the Archduke Philip of Burgundy, no doubt discussing with him various proposed marriage alliances near St. Peter's Church just outside Calais. Henry travelled in great pomp wanting to impress, and there were jousts, pageantry and gay music whilst he was there.

They returned home in June to find the plague had done its worst, killing 20,000 people. The summer days passed quickly at Greenwich Palace, but they had to endure a great sorrow with the death of Prince Edmond only a few months old. The infant was buried in the shrine of St. Edward in Westminster Abbey together with their infant daughter Elizabeth.

VIII   HENRY'S PART IN CABOT'S VOYAGES

Henry VII never held any desire to extend England's territory or for foreign aggrandizement, yet with his customary sagacity he realized the importance of discovery and exploration in unknown lands. Oceanic discovery became a central part of the king's policy in the 1490s. It is not, perhaps, widely known that the king was the patron of John Cabot and his three sons, Sebastian, Ludovico and Sancio. John was a skilled cartographer and master mariner, the greatest of the Cabots.

It is possible, but extremely unlikely that John Cabot was born in England.[1] According to J.A. Williamson, an authority on the voyages of the Cabots, John Cabot was probably a Genoese by birth, but it is certain that in 1476 he became a naturalized citizen of Venice.[2] His wife was a Venetian. Sebastian, the most celebrated of the Cabots after his father John, was born in Venice about 1483-6 and brought to England by his father about 1490. Actually John in his Venetian period began his remarkable career as a merchant engaged in the spice trade by the ancient route through the Levant. It was an early encounter with Asiatic dealers that fired John's enthusiasm for a direct westward expedition across the Atlantic to the east coast of Asia. Whether John Cabot ever knew Christopher Columbus is not known, though in this great age of discovery Columbus would have been making his first transatlantic voyage in 1492-3 prior to Cabot's voyages.

In 1496 or earlier John Cabot was living in Bristol, and on 5 March Henry VII at Westminster published letters patent to the effect that Cabot and his three sons, including their heirs and deputies, were empowered to sail under the English flag with five ships to all parts of the eastern, western and northern sea to discover all lands hitherto unknown to Christians. They were to bear the whole cost of the venture themselves, but to pay the king one fifth of the profits accruing from each voyage. It was ordained that the mariners were to be exempt from customs on goods brought back by them.

With regard to the bulls of Pope Alexander VI already partitioning the unknown parts of the globe between Spain and Portugal, Henry VII was prepared to respect the rights of other powers and to acknowledge them, but no more than this.

70

On 2 May 1497, John Cabot set sail with a crew of eighteen men in the *The Matthew* and on 24 June landed on a coast which he thought to be that of Asia, though it was almost certainly Newfoundland or Nova Scotia. It is unfortunate that John Cabot's journal has not been preserved, like the journal of Columbus. He certainly observed that the land was occupied, though he did not see any of the people. On 6 August Cabot returned to Bristol. His expedition had been a success, for he had developed for England a new and wealthy trade, thus delighting the king.

He was received with enthusiasm at Henry's court, given a private audience by the king, who granted him a gratuity of £10 and later an annual pension of £20. Everybody greeted him as 'the great admiral'.[3] Cabot dressed in choice silks basked in his success. The Milanese ambassador informs us that enormous numbers of codfish were to be caught on the banks of Newfoundland, where previously England had been dependent on the Iceland fishery.

John Cabot made a second voyage during May 1498, a fully equipped trading expedition with cargoes of English goods to be bartered for the spices of Cathay. He left Bristol with five ships, but one of these was damaged by tempests and was compelled to return to Ireland. Precise information about this voyage is lacking, but it is evident that Cabot sailed up the American coastline west and south for a considerable distance, thus arousing Spain's alarm at England's rivalry. However, Cabot's ambition to sail to cities mightier than Venice, to a kind of glorious Cathay of Marco Polo, remained an empty dream. On the 1498 expedition, Henry VII contributed a large ship, manned, victualled and equipped, and was prepared to advance loans to the merchants of London and Bristol. There is evidence of Henry's strong interest in these Cabot voyages in his carefully kept privy purse expenses. Incentives and rewards were given to merchants, who had ventured to the new land (Newfoundland), to a priest, who was travelling there and to explorers, who returned with eagles, hawks and popinjays.

The 1490s were great years for Portuguese explorers, such as the celebrated Vasco da Gama, who made his pioneer voyage across the Indian Ocean in 1499. Among Portuguese explorers was João Fernandez, who may have accompanied the nobleman's Gaspar Corte Real in his voyage northwards to rediscover Greenland. We know that Fernandez was in England in early 1501 and informed King Henry VII of the discovery of Greenland.[4] It is curious that Henry later, during March 1501, issued letters patent to João Fernandez and to two other Portuguese, Francisco Fernandez and João Gonsalvez, also to three merchants of Bristol, Richard Warde, Thomas Asshehurst and John Thomas, to sail the seas without any impediment, and to annex heathen lands hitherto unknown to all Christians.

It is amusing to relate, according to the London Chronicles and John Cabot's own account, that after one of his expeditions in 1502 he brought home three savages, Alonquin Indians, whom he had captured, and presented them to Henry VII in the Palace of Westminster.[5] Henry's curiosity was certainly aroused. 'These were clothed in beasts skins and dide eate raw flesh and speke such speech that no man could understand them and in their demeanour like to bruit beastes, whom the King kept a time after'.

One of Henry VII's objects in encouraging voyages of discovery was to find a short way to the Indies. His interest was certainly not confined to motives of curiosity, nor to making Christian converts. Later during his reign, the king rewarded Sebastian Cabot with a pension of £10 per annum, not for having made discoveries, but 'in consideration of diligent service and attendance ... in and about our Town and port of Bristol'. Sebastian invented the logbook and this fine seaman also made methodical experiments and observations concerning the needle. He had the reputation for being economical with the truth and his character lacked integrity.

During the last year of the first Tudor king's life (1509), in the spring, Sebastian was at last given the opportunity to sail on a voyage from Bristol. Later he claimed that the expedition led to the discovery of the North-West Passage. Sebastian was aided by the king and embarked in two ships, making for the coast of Labrador, already explored by previous navigators. Sebastian thought he was making for Cathay. The voyage was extremely hazardous since the sea abounded with floating ice. Unfortunately the seamen mutinied and Sebastian was compelled to turn back. It seems almost certain that Sebastian prior to this penetrated Fox Channel, before turning south into Hudson Bay. He certainly sailed down the Atlantic coast of the 'New Found Land' and parts of the coast of what constitutes the present United States. Then he sailed to England only to find that his patron Henry VII had died on 22 April (1509). He tried to interest Henry's son, who succeeded him as Henry VIII, but that young monarch was more interested in conquests in Europe than exploring the North-West Passage or financing a further venture.

Frustrated, Sebastian then served Ferdinand of Spain.

Most recent historians and others accused Sebastian of being a shameless liar. If indeed he claimed much of the credit for many of his father's achievements, he was guilty of a distortion of the truth. It is far from certain that he sailed with his father to North America in 1497.

IX HENRY AND RELATIONS WITH IRELAND

Henry VII partly owed his success as a statesman to his shrewd judgment and to his wise choice of deputies. Sir Edward Poynings, for instance, whom the king had known when exiled in Brittany, was an excellent appointment as Lord Deputy in Ireland, at a salary of £500 per annum. As a young man he had taken an important part in the Kentish rising during the Buckingham rebellion and later in 1485 joined Henry when he landed at Milford Haven.[1]

The king's title of 'Lord of Ireland' after Bosworth is somewhat misleading because he became 'Lord of Ireland' only in name. To Henry the native Irish were savage, several centuries behind the times.

As already mentioned, the Anglo-Irish were Yorkist supporters, inimical to Henry's title as Lancastrian heir. The Butlers, created earls of Ormond, were the only Anglo-Irish to support the king. In Henry's reign the English land was understood to be the Pale, or four counties of Dublin, Kildare, Louth and Meath, besides southern Wexford and a few towns and cities such as Dublin, Drogheda, and Waterford, which were always pro-English. A large part of the country on the other hand had returned to the old native princes, since the earldoms of Desmond, Kildare and Ormonde covered most of Munster, and a large part of Leinster. Ancient English families were predominant in most of Connaught and eastern Ulster.

One difficulty was that most kings of England had avoided travelling to Ireland, the exceptions being of the medieval King John during 1210, and King Richard II during the early 1390s and his famous visit in 1399 before his deposition.

As an administrator, Poynings was invaluable to the king being instrumental in defeating the Yorkist faction and calming Ireland. By the end of 1495 Henry's reputation had grown apace on the continent. Edward Poynings is most memorable in Irish history for the measures passed in the parliament that he summoned to Drogheda on 1 December 1494. His main incentive and object was to restore the royal authority, which had been paramount 200 years earlier under Edward I. He also dealt with dangerous opponents and various abuses. In organizing the Pale as a garrison acting in English interests, Sir Edmund was as successful as he was in sterilizing the Dublin parliament.

The Drogheda Parliament passed forty-nine Acts, some of considerable importance. They are often referred to as 'Poynings Laws' and concerned the government, the parliament, the law, the revenue and the armed forces. Edmund Curtis has discussed them in detail in a chapter in *Henry VII's Relations with Scotland and Ireland.*[2]

Henry VII eventually made his peace with Gerald Fitzgerald, eighth earl of Kildare, 'uncrowned' King of Ireland in earlier times. He was invited to England, his attainder reversed in the English parliament and enjoyed amicable relations with King Henry, who provided him with a wife, his second cousin Elizabeth St. John. Kildare eventually returned to Ireland, no longer a rebel, but enjoying Henry's support and in a position of great authority. On 25 March 1498, a commission was published for Kildare to hold a parliament. Henry was content because his lordship of Ireland had been restored.

X PRINCE ARTHUR'S MARRIAGE
WITH SPAIN

King Henry VII's most cherished desire was for his son and heir Arthur Prince of Wales to marry Catherine of Aragon, youngest daughter of Isabella of Castile and her husband Ferdinand of Aragon. With his political foresight, Henry glimpsed Spain's future greatness in the sixteenth century. He realized that the Spanish marriage would seal the public recognition of his dynasty, to admit him to that circle of royalty which was beginning to dominate Europe, for Catherine had the royal blood of the Plantagenets, being a descendant of John of Gaunt and his father Edward III. Isabella and Ferdinand were also pleased, reassured by their able residential ambassador in England Dr. Rodrigo Gonsalez de Puebla that King Henry was, by 1500, master of his kingdom, having gained victory over the main Pretenders and consolidated his rule. No longer was the dim-witted earl of Warwick a menace, for he had been executed in 1499. For thirteen arduous years since 1487, de Puebla had laboured and negotiated for the marriage, worming his way into the confidence of King Henry and assuring Ferdinand and Isabella that alliance with the King of England would be profitable to Spain.

Many of de Puebla's contemporaries were openly critical and contemptuous of the Spanish ambassador, and his posthumous reputation has consequently suffered.[1] The more aristocratic members of the Catholic monarch's advisers sneered at de Puebla'a humble birth and his habit of sponging on others.

His reputation is largely biased and unfair because de Puebla regarded his chief mission in England to be the preservation of the English alliance and for twenty years he worked hard to achieve harmonious relations between England and Spain. His relations with Henry VII were on the whole excellent so that the Spanish became suspicious of Henry's intimacy with de Puebla and of the ambassador's alleged pro-English sentiments. He never concealed his admiration for the first Tudor king's ability, his political wisdom and indeed agreed with Henry on many points of foreign policy, urging them on Ferdinand almost as if he was foreign secretary.

Dr. Gustav Bergenroth in his introduction to the *Calendar of State Papers, Spanish* gives a one-sided pen-portrait of de Puebla, an unfair one.

He describes him as:

> an abject, pettifogging rascal, a shady trickster ... a shabby and deformed little cripple, mean, boastful, shameless ... without anything to commend him to the rulers of Spain and England except servility, low cunning and a complete lack of moral scruples.

If Bergenroth's estimate of de Puebla is true, how did it come about that Ferdinand and Isabella of Spain deeply respected de Puebla's ability and used the most flattering language when corresponding with him?[2] Above everything, de Puebla prized his ambassadorial dignity and deeply resented Ayala when he came to England.

It was owing to de Puebla's contemporary Don Pedro de Ayala, sometime Spanish ambassador in Edinburgh, who was directly responsible for derogatory reports about his fellow diplomat. Don Pedro, like de Puebla, was a churchman, otherwise he was his opposite in character. Where de Puebla was of humble origin, Don Pedro was an aristocrat, with charming manners, witty, amusing and suave, though his ignorance of law and Latin was profound. He was a successful ambassador in Scotland, becoming a great friend of James IV, indeed was responsible for turning Perkin Warbeck out of Scotland, for he influenced James against him. When he later came to England, he became very friendly with Henry VII, who enjoyed his company and hunted and gamed with him. Henry took malicious pleasure in playing Don Pedro off against de Puebla and whetting his jealousy of his rival. De Puebla was unfairly despised for lacking *limpieza de sangue* (pureness of blood) and for his Jewish blood, although many of Ferdinand's and Isabella's most able servants were Jews. Both de Puebla and Don Pedro constantly intrigued against one another. Don Pedro de Ayala spread the false rumour that King Henry was not serious about the proposed match between Arthur and Catherine, and was thinking of marrying his eldest son to Margaret of Austria.

For as long as she could remember, Catherine had been taught to think of herself as the Princess of Wales. Of Isabella's daughters, she bore a more striking physical resemblance to her mother than her elder sisters Maria and Joanna. Her character was also similar to Queen Isabella's in many respects, her gracious dignity, her marked intelligence, her earnestness, and pride of birth. We are so accustomed to think of the Spanish princess as Shakespeare's dowdy matron in his *Henry VIII*, but she was an extremely pretty and attractive girl when fifteen and about to marry Arthur. Michel Sittow's portrait of her with light brown hair almost golden, her large expressive dark eyes, her dainty limbs and the graceful way she moved, provides a far more accurate impression. Of Prince Arthur we do not know much, he was studious and intellectual like his father, an over-tall fair boy of fourteen in the autumn of 1501, not athletic, like his younger brother Henry and not fit enough for jousting, as he was never really robust.

Catherine's dowry was fixed at 200,000 crowns by the marriage settlement, 100,000 to be paid on the wedding day, 50,000 more within six months and the final fifty thousand within a year. The valuable jewels and plate the Spanish bride brought with her were valued at 35,000 crowns and were to lead to bitter disputes. Catalina, as she was called in Spain, had been born in Alcala de Henares, a Castilian village near Madrid, in December 1485. Her earliest memories may well have been of Granada, that most lovely Spanish city and its Alhambra, which her parents, their Catholic Majesties, entered jubilantly when the last Moorish king was forced to abandon it. Catholic Spain had triumphed over the Moors. Catalina was barely six and always retained a special love for Granada. Her elder sister Isabella married Alfonso of Portugal, only to be widowed at the age of twenty, while another sister Joanna was to be wedded to Philip the Emperor Maximilian's son, a brilliant marriage for Philip enjoyed great wealth and importance.

There is an excellent account of Princess Catherine's journey to England to marry Arthur Prince of Wales in J. Leland's works:[3]

The agreement between the noble Kings of England and Spaine, for a marriage between the Princess Katheryn Daughter of the said King of Spaine, and Arthur Prince of Wales, being prefixed and concluded, the said Princess with a sufficient guard and nobles of her country assigned as her conductors and assistants went on board a navy of shipps, prepared for carrying her to England ...

The count of Cabra, well known for his prowess in the Granadan wars, commanded her escort, and other Spanish grandees accompanied her, such as Alonzo de Fonseca, archbishop of Santiago and the bishop of Majorca. Her permanent household consisted of sixty people, including Catherine's formidable Doña Elvira Manuel, her severe duenna. Leland relates that the party encountered many jeopardies from storms and tempests ... they were at length conveyed into the English ports and fortunately arrived at Plymouth, far in the west country, where the Princess and her attendants landed on Saturday 2 October 1501. To the cheering of warm English hearts, she passed through the city, and Catherine, despite later misfortunes, never lost her popularity. In Exeter, she was officially welcomed by Lord Willoughby de Broke, high steward of the king's household, also by Richmond King-at-Arms and other heralds.

Dr. de Puebla should have travelled to the west country to welcome the Spanish Princess, but Don Pedro de Ayala had successfully intrigued against his colleague and coming to England formed one of the party escorting Catherine to London. The jovial, witty Ayala was an amusing escort, and very congenial to Henry VII, with whom he hunted and played at dice.[4]

King Henry at Richmond in Surrey in his curiosity to meet the princess, attended by a great company rode to Easthampstead where Arthur joined him. Meanwhile Princess Catherine and her company had moved from Andover and Basingstoke to the bishop of Bath's Palace at Dogmersfield not far from London Bridge. Spanish etiquette forbade a high-born Spanish bride to raise her veil or allow her face to be seen before the final benediction had been granted at her wedding. Both Doña Elvira, her duenna, and the archbishop of Santiago were determined to adhere to this custom. However, they did not know Henry. He was the master in his kingdom and was determined to see his son's bride, and nothing could deter him. He turned to his lords, exclaiming in a loud voice, 'My lords, a council, we shall meet at Dogmersfield'. Then he set off at a gallop, while the gay Don Pedro, hardly able to conceal his laughter, and the various lords followed at a more leisurely pace.

At Dogmersfield, the Spanish councillors headed by the archbishop of Toledo, the count of Cabra and the bishop of Malaga gravely told the king that Princess Catherine was resting and could see nobody. 'Tell the lords of Spain,' said Henry, dogmatically, 'I will see the Princess, even were she in her bed.' Doña Elvira was deeply disapproving. Henry was very impressed by the shy, beautiful girl, who curtsied to him. How did they correspond? The king spoke French, but hardly knew any Spanish, while Catherine did not understand French and knew no English. It is possible they conversed in Latin.

According to Leland's account,[5] after Henry had supped, he with the Prince Arthur:

> full courteously visited the lady in her owne chamber, and then she and her ladyes called for their minstrels and with right goodly Behavious and manner solaced themselves with the Disports of Dancing.

Catherine loved dancing when a girl and indeed throughout her life. Prince Arthur also danced with the Lady Guildford (his sister Mary's governess), 'right pleasantly and honourably'. Now he wrote to his future father-in-law Ferdinand and Isabella that he had never felt so much joy in his life as when he beheld the sweet face of his bride. No woman in the world could be more agreeable to him. He promised to make a good husband.

After leaving Dogsmerfield, the king repaired to Easthampstead and then to Richmond where we can be sure he told his queen his impressions of their future daughter-in-law. 'He finally entered his barge and was carried to his lodging called Barnard's Castle,' according to Leland's account,[6] 'while the Queene's Grace, ... repaired hither in her Barge by water, to be ready for inducting the noble Princess of Spaine...'

It was at Kingston-on-Thames, then a mere village, that Catherine met for the first time one of the most powerful courtiers in England, Edward Stafford duke of Buckingham, a young nobleman aged twenty-three. He was on horseback, surrounded by 300 or 400 of his gentlemen and yeomen, all dressed in his livery of black and red. He has been described as handsome, charming, extravagant, a little stupid with too exalted an estimate of the privileges attaching to his rank. He was Catherine's first friend in England, an aristrocrat like herself, and the friendship would endure until his execution during the early reign of Henry VIII.

Arthur and Catherine were given a magnificent wedding, for Henry knew he must spare no expense, but the City of London and the nobility were compelled to pay much of the cost. Trumpets and the booming of cannons greeted Catherine as she moved from the riverside to the bishop's palace. All kinds of quaint devices that the Londoners could invent brightened the streets, gay with triumphal arches. They were married in St. Paul's by the archbishop of Canterbury, Henry Deane, formerly bishop of Salisbury,[7] who had temporarily succeeded Morton on his death. It was Henry duke of York, a robust boy aged ten, who gave his right hand to the bride as she walked up the church. After the ceremony there was the clanging of all the bells in London, and the conduits spouted wine. People shouted so heartily that they became hoarse.

Leland's *Collecteana*[8] gives the fullest and most interesting account of the 'Jousts, banquetts and Disguisings used at the intertayment of Katherine, wife to Prince Arthure, eldest son to King Henry VII. Upon Thursdaye,' it relates,

> the great and large voide space before Westminster Hall and the Palace was gravelled sanded and goodly ordered for the Ease of the Hurses, and a tilt sett and arraysed at the whole length from the Watergate well nighe up to the entrance of the Gate that openeth unto the Kings Street towards the Sanctuary ...
>
> As soone as Dynner was done in the court, the Queene's grace, my lade the Kinge's mother and her sister, with many other ladyes and gentlewomen of Honor, to the number of two or three hundred, entered into this goodly and well prepared stage, and after that the

King's Highnes himselfe, with his noble issue, the Prince and the duke of Yorke, the Earle of Oxford, Great Chamberlene of England, the Earl of Derbye, Constable of the said Realme ...

and many other lords. Nobody was more resplendent than the duke of Buckingham 'in his pavilion of white and greene silk, being foure square, having proper turrets and pynacles of curious work, sett full of redd roses of the King's badges'.

Mention is made of the 'pleasant disguising and subtile pageants. The first was a castle right cunningly devised, sett upon wheels, and drawne into the said Hall by Fower great beasts with chaines of golde'. Henry wanted to impress the courts of Europe with this spectacle and pageantry. The walls of Westminster Hall were 'richly hanged' by the king's command with 'pleasant clothes of Arras'. Young Henry duke of York (afterwards Henry VIII) seems to have enjoyed himself, dancing:

> two Bais daunces with his sister the Lady Margaret. He amused the company when he perceiving himself to be accombred with his clothes, suddenly cast off his gowne, and daunced in his jackett with the said Lady Margaret in so goodly and pleasant a manner, that it was to the King and Queene a great and singular pleasure.[9]

Lady Margaret Beaufort gave a lavish dinner in honour of the Spanish grandees in her town house 'Coldharbour'.

Arthur Prince of Wales was the nominal head of a Council in Ludlow on the borders of Wales, and it was in towering Ludlow Castle that he and his bride were to live for the next five months. Among members of his Council were Sir Richard Pole, an able administrator. There in Ludlow Castle, the Welsh magnates paid their homage to the young Prince and Princess of Wales. There came Rhys ap Thomas, called by King Henry 'Father Rhys', bearded and courtly. We can imagine the vast hall of the castle where the ill-fated sons of Edward IV had once witnessed the smoke issuing from the great hearths, insufficient to warm Arthur and Catherine. There would be the music of the sweet-voiced Welsh harpists singing their ancient ballads. Five brief months, then the sweating sickness came to Ludlow during March 1502. Whether Arthur died from it or from 'consumption' we cannot be certain, but he died on 2 April, for he had always been delicate. He was not yet sixteen.

The earl of Surrey represented King Henry as chief mourner at the Prince of Wales's magnificent funeral in Worcester Cathedral. According to one eye witness, it occurred on 'the foulest, cold windy and rainy day I have ever seen'. Catherine did not attend it, lying ill in Ludlow, and many weeks passed before she was well enough to be borne slowly in a litter into the presence of the queen at Richmond.

Immediately after the prince had died, Sir Richard Pole sent letters to King Henry at Greenwich with the heaving tidings. His Council not daring to impart the tragic news to Henry, entrusted the distasteful duty to the king's 'ghostly Father Confessor'. He knocked at the King's Chamber and when permitted to enter told the king in these words: '*Si bona de manu deir suscipimus, male antem quare sustineamus* (if we have received good things by the hand of God, where (why) should we not also receive misfortune.[10] Then he told the king of the death of his dearest son.

It was a devastating blow for Henry and Elizabeth, but the affectionate manner in which he related the dreadful intelligence to his queen reveals not only his tact, but the loving relation he had attained with her. Elizabeth, too, comforted her husband, beseeching his grace to remember the weal of his own noble person, the comfort of his realm and of her. God had left him 'a fayre Prince and two fayre Princesses. God is where He was, and we are both young enough'. (Henry was about forty-five at this time). However, when she reached her chamber, Elizabeth collapsed, overcome with grief. It was now Henry's turn to comfort her, telling how what 'wise counsell she had given him before and he for his parte would thank God for his sonne and would she do likewise'.

Arthur's death affected the close relations Henry had established with Ferdinand and Isabella, for they were to deteriorate. Five weeks later, Ferdinand and Isabella ordered an ambassador Duque de Estrada to demand the immediate return of Catherine together with the 100,000 crowns already paid and the portion due to her on her marriage. He wanted to arrange, if possible, a marriage between his widowed daughter and Henry, the only surviving son of Henry VII and Elizabeth his queen. The king was fearful for his dynasty, realizing the risk that it might not last.

Catherine's duenna Doña Elvira was adamant that the princess's marriage had never been consummated, and all the ladies of her household were prepared to swear that she was *virgo intacta*. She was very angry with Dr. de Puebla for at first declaring the opposite, and the Spanish ambassador was forced to make an ignominious apology. He now wrote the new version to the sovereigns of Spain. Even after more than nearly five centuries there remains a slight doubt as to the truth. Catherine had been influenced against de Puebla by Don Pedro de Ayala, the charming diplomat, and in her letters to her parents the princess attacked de Puebla unfairly.

Henry had no intention whatsoever of relinquishing the 100,000 crowns of Catherine's dowry, and he had the right to a further payment of 100,000 crowns before she could claim her dower settlements. During her widowhood, she was living in the vast palace of the bishop of Durham in the Strand, a centre of Spanish intrigue, for Spanish courtiers swarmed about its corridors. Her main troubles for the next few years concerned her financial problems, and both Henry and her father Ferdinand were niggardly in providing her with financial assistance, Henry excusing himself on the grounds that she did not have to maintain such a vast staff. He certainly lacked generosity, loving riches above most things. Eventually, however, Henry did allow her £100 a month, directing his councillor William Holybrand to see that nothing was wasted and to keep strict accounts.

If Catherine was ever to marry Henry, soon to be Prince of Wales, it would encounter serious difficulties. A chapter in Leviticus (18:16) forbade a man to marry his brother's wife. It was also necessary for a papal dispensation to remove the canonical impediments and a papal bull was very slow in its preparation. Pope Alexander VI died about 1503 without giving the required dispensation, and Julius II seemed to doubt his authority in this matter.

Ten months after the death of Prince Arthur, weary with childbearing there died in the Tower of London on 11 February 1503 – her thirty-seventh birthday – Queen Elizabeth of York, much beloved by the people. It was a grievous loss for Henry VII, and for a while he withdrew into a private place with a few attendants and would see nobody. Her body lay in state in the chapel of the Tower, and then taken in procession to Westminster Abbey for burial. There in the beautiful chapel of Henry VII she lies resplendent beside her husband. Polydore Vergil, in his *Anglia Historia* wrote of Elizabeth:

> She was a woman of such a character that it be hard to judge whether she displayed more of majesty and dignity in her life than wisdom and moderation.

Thomas More also wrote a powerful memorial elegy on her death, for he had known her well and admired her character.

XI PRINCESS MARGARET'S WEDDING

One of King Henry's wisest actions was to marry his elder daughter Margaret Tudor during 1503 to James IV of Scotland. It was a sterling example of the king's admirable slow and patient statecraft, considering James's consistent hostility, having memorable and beneficial consequences in the ultimate union of the kingdoms of England and Scotland.[1] Margaret's great-grandson James VI of Scotland became King of England in 1603. It is usually said of Henry that he lacked imagination. Is it possible, however, that the king *did* foresee such an occasion with the death without issue of his surviving son's children?

When it was objected in Council that were the king's sons to die without issue then the kingdom of England would fall to the kingdom of Scotland, the king shrewdly replied that:

> if should be, Scotland would be an accession to England and not England to Scotland, for that the greater would draw the less, and that it was a safer union than that of France.

Princess Margaret was a special favourite of her grandmother the Lady Margaret Beaufort, who left her in her will 'a gyrdell of gold conteyning XXIX linkes, with a grete pomander at oon ende'. January 1502 marked the formal betrothal of the king's eldest daughter to James IV. Both the king's mother and the queen wanted to delay the marriage until Margaret was 18, but she was only 14 when during July 1503 her father the king took her to say farewell to her grandmother at Collyweston in Northamptonshire on her way to her wedding in Scotland. She was very nobly accompanied on the long journey, riding on 'a faire palfrey, her saddle wrought with red roses.'[2] On the way to Edinburgh, her longest stay was in York, where some miles from that city she was received by the fifth earl of Northumberland and conducted to the minster to hear mass. The Northumberlands, attended by several hundred retainers, escorted her across the border leaving her with the earl and countess of Surrey, who escorted her through Haddington to Dalkeith and then Edinburgh. There she would meet her husband.

Margaret was self-willed, accustomed from infancy to get her own way, like most princesses. She had been carefully educated at the medieval Eltham Palace near London where one of her brother Henry's tutors was the learned John Skelton. On one occasion in 1500 Thomas More brought the famous scholar and humanist Desiderius Erasmus to be received at Eltham by the royal children. Margaret lacked the grace and beauty of her younger sister Mary, her father's favourite, with her golden hair and lovely figure.

He had planned her slow progress northwards to stress the wealth and glory of his dynasty. It was from the first a political marriage.

James IV and his bride were married during November in Holyrood Chapel. There was a discrepancy in their years, for James was already over thirty while Margaret was only fourteen, so they were hardly suited as companions. The King of Scotland had many mistresses, including Lady Margaret Drummond to whom he was deeply attached. Yet James did his utmost to please her, passing his evenings in her apartments, playing at cards with her and giving rewards to the musicians and dancers who performed in her presence. Margaret loved music, like her father, and played the lute and the clavichord.[3] At first the young Queen of Scotland pined for her homeland and her father's court. Later, she slowly warmed to her husband.

She wrote to her father: that my lord of Surrey enjoyed too much of her husband's favour and was constantly with him. 'I would I were with your grace now, and many times have, I would answer'.[4] She was at first desperately unhappy. She did not like her husband's prickly beard, and James jokingly had it removed. He was attractive as a man, singing to the lute, and it was mostly Margaret's fault that she was not happier, being headstrong and flighty by nature.

Henry could occasionally be generous, sending his son-in-law a present of 5,000 marks to defray the cost of his daughter's journey. After she had reached the border, James was responsible for the expenses.

Margaret had a passion for jewellery — her father prudently collected it as an investment – and knowing this left her a valuable legacy of jewels later withheld by Henry VIII.[5]

The first Tudor king was justly praised for the patience and wisdom he had shown in uniting 'The Thrissil and the Rois[6] (the Rose), no small achievement when we consider the long years of enmity between the two countries. Yet it persisted in 1508 when Henry was compelled to send Dr. Nicholas West to the Scottish court to prevent, if possible, a renewal of the ancient league between France and Scotland: Scotland was strongly on the side of France and opposed England at this juncture. In the intervening years, however, James, wanting to cultivate the good will of his father-in-

Henry Tudor as a young man. Mid-sixteenth century drawing by Jacques le Boucq.

Henry VII in the transept window of Great Malvern Priory Church.

Queen Elizabeth of York by an unknown artist.

Arthur, Prince of Wales (1486-1502) by an unknown artist.

Catherine of Aragon by Michel Sittow.

Henry VII's chapel in Westminster Abbey showing roof vaulting.

Tomb effigies of Henry VII and Queen Elizabeth by Pietro Torrigiano in Westminster Abbey.

Effigy of Henry VII by Pietro Torrigiano in Westminster Abbey.

law, sent him presents 'of a great number of good hawks', and of Scotch horses, principally from Galloway, so that by such mutual tokens and propines (presents) the love and beauty and kindness was maintained and cherished 'betwixt the father and the son'.

There is very little evidence that Henry considered marrying the widowed Catherine of Aragon, as mentioned mostly with horror by several historians. Isabella would have preferred her daughter to return to Spain. Yet he was acutely aware of the insecurity in the kingdom now that only Henry duke of York survived and his two daughters. Edmund and Arthur were both dead. Indeed, Henry considered remarriage with a number of ladies. Isabella of Castile suggested that he should marry the young Queen of Naples and during 1504 when Henry was forty-seven, he seemed to favour the match. He wanted assurances about the personal attraction of the lady, whether her teeth were good, whether her figure was plump and whether voice and face were pleasing to the ear and eye. So he sent ambassadors to report whether her breath was sweet. To do so, it was vital to get as near as possible to her.

Another candidate was the widowed Louise duchess of Savoy, but Henry received such a detailed and favourable report about the queen of Naples from his envoys that Bacon wrote of him that if Henry 'had been young, a man would have judged him to be amorous'. However, the king did not consider her possessions or revenues sufficient and he was aware of her dependence on the goodwill of Ferdinand of Aragon and his queen.

Henry's marriage to Elizabeth of York had been affectionate, he had grown fond of her, but deprived of her he experienced the sense of insecurity dogging his years of exile. There is no doubt that his character deteriorated. He became more grasping, more stingy, more melancholy and except for his love for his mother, seemed to his courtiers curiously remote and cold.

The earl of Derby, married to Henry's mother, always remained loyal to the king after 1485, unlike his younger brother William. He had given Henry valuable support at the battle of Stoke near Newark and the king handsomely rewarded him by granting him in tail male (to descend only to male heirs) the Lancashire estates of Sir Thomas Broughton, Lord Lovel and Sir Thomas Pilkington and also some lands which had descended to James Herrington, who later became dean of York.

Five months after the execution of Sir William Stanley (1495), the king, probably to show Derby his good will, together with his queen had visited the earl and countess at Lathom in Lancashire. The royal couple rode north to Winwick to be welcomed by the rector James Stanley, Derby's younger son, and then on to Lathom to be lavishly entertained for five days.[7] Henry had insatiable curiosity about the estates of his most powerful subjects, consequently he inspected his son-in-law's entire estate. Legend has it that he was peering over a flat roof when he heard Derby's jester whisper in the earl's ear, 'Tom, remember Will'. The king hastily retreated downstairs to the society of his mother.

The king and queen stayed at Knowsley in a suite of rooms subsequently known as the Royal Lodgings in the present south wing of the Hall. When George Strange, Derby's heir, who had escaped execution ordered by Richard III at Bosworth, died during December 1503, five months before his father, some said he had been poisoned.

A far more important death on 26 November 1504 was that of Isabella of Castile, the Catholic queen, in her castle overlooking Medina del Campo. It would affect the Anglo-Spanish alliance in a marked way, for relations between the two countries deteriorated. The question of the succession to Castile became a problem. Isabella's son was dead, so by right, it now descended to Joanna, Catherine's elder sister and wife of the Archduke Philip the Handsome of the Netherlands, son of the Emperor Maximilian, not to Ferdinand of Aragon, Isabella's consort.

A mere three days before her death, Isabella had added a codicil to her will:

> If Juana, my dearly loved daughter, heiress and lawful successor (to Castile) should be absent from this realm, or if having come thither she should depart from it no matter when and should wish to live elsewhere or if being here she should lack the desire or the ability to rule or to administer it, then Ferdinand was to rule, govern and administer it in his daughter's name.

Joanna was a tragic character, like a leading personality in a Greek drama, doomed to be vilely betrayed by her own father, husband and others, who cared not for her, but only for her inheritance.[8]

When aged sixteen, she had been betrothed by her parents to Philip the Handsome of Burgundy, a political marriage designed by Isabella and Ferdinand to increase Spain's dynastic prestige and to increase her influence at foreign courts. Joanna was the most beautiful of her family, so it is really no wonder that when Henry VII briefly met her at his court at Windsor that his senses were stirred. She was very accomplished, spoke several languages, an excellent dancer, and played the clavichord. Her misfortune was to be completely neurotic, subject to hysterical outbursts, and a prey to long spells of melancholy mingled with moods of wild gaiety. She fell passionately in love with her husband Philip, but her possessive craving for him first amused then maddened her husband, who was of shallow character. Her wild jealousy of his mistresses led her to cut off the long golden tresses of hair of a hated rival mistress with a pair of scissors. Indeed, her moods were as variable as the English climate. Her father would later openly declare that his daughter was mad. Blind to her husband's faults, although she sometimes hated him, after his early death she would insist on carrying about his body in a coffin.

Henry VII was later to consider marriage with her, never believing Ferdinand's talk of her madness. It was not only the knowledge that she was Queen of Castile that weighed with him as a major inducement. He was responsive to beauty and distress, and pitied her for her loneliness and sadness.

He had not always enjoyed harmonious relations with the Archduke Philip. When he imposed an import duty on cloth, Henry VII wrote on 26 June 1496 a dignified letter of protest to the archduke's Council.[9] Eventually, the duty was withdrawn. Henry was eager for intimate political relations with the Emperor Maximilian and Archduke Philip, loaning them large sums of money.

During early January 1506, the Archduke Philip decided to go to Spain with a huge fleet, but a great gale rose during the voyage along the Atlantic coast for 42 hours. The expedition confronted mighty perils. Only Queen Joanna seemed impervious to the dangers, even exultant, as her arms tightened about her husband's knees. At last the battered ship bearing Philip and Joanna reached the shallow harbour of Melcombe Regis, near Weymouth in Dorset. At first mistaken for a pirate, Philip was soon recognized and invited to King Henry's court then at Windsor, on 31 January. Joanna did not accompany Philip then. She only appeared at Henry's court on 10 February.

Henry knew well how to entertain his visitors with magnificent displays and he treated Philip with courtesy in Windsor Castle. They got on very well together, hunting deer in the forest, playing tennis and hawking. The secret Treaty of Windsor was signed, a treaty of alliance.[10] Henry promised to assist the cause of the Habsburgs in Spain by recognizing Philip as King of Castile. He was now hostile to Ferdinand and wished to undermine his position in Castile. An important clause of the agreement concerned Edmund de la Pole, earl of Suffolk, a rebel in exile. Henry insisted that Suffolk should be brought to Calais on 16 March, handed over to the English garrison and then escorted to Dover and the Tower of London where he was to remain Henry's close prisoner for a few years and executed by Henry VIII in 1513. The Emperor Maximilian welcomed the possibility of a marriage between his daughter Margaret of Savoy and Henry, but the lady firmly declined the proposed match, preferring to remain a widow.

Everybody enjoyed the revelry in Windsor Castle, even Catherine of Aragon, eager to get away from Durham House. She danced in the great hall with two of her ladies, jewels sparkling in her hair, while Henry's youngest daughter Mary played the lute very well. When Catherine asked Philip to show the company one of the Spanish dances he declined, saying he was a mariner, referring to his recent shipwreck experience, and yet you would make me dance. He preferred not to be a gallant, so that he could discuss political matters with King Henry. Catherine, longing to see her sister Joanna to confide her troubles to her, was deeply disappointed when she only saw her briefly. Joanna was no longer the gay, high-spirited girl she remembered, but a sad, tormented, tearful creature, unhappy because her husband preferred other women. Henry, however, was impressed with her and wanted to see more of her. She was soon sent back to Plymouth in a litter by her husband. Knowing that Catherine was writing to Joanna soon after her departure, the king asked her to say that he had been very pleased by her brief visit, and much regretted that it had not been longer.

Philip's relations with his father-in-law Ferdinand of Aragon had been acrimonious and bitter, but they were reconciled during July 1506. Ferdinand assured Philip that Joanna was unfit to rule Castile and that he favoured his son-in-law acting as Regent and assuming all her duties. In reality he himself wanted to be King of Castile. So he cunningly persuaded Philip to sign an agreement appointing him an executor. Then Philip suddenly died on 25 September, possibly owing to over-exertion after a meal, and Joanna became a broken-hearted widow. Their son the Archduke Charles was later to be the powerful Emperor Charles V. Maximilian, the boy's grandfather, began proposing in September negotiations for a marriage between the Archduke Charles and Mary Tudor, Henry's youngest daughter. Though seriously considered, nothing eventually came of this proposed match.

Henry's thoughts now turned to a possible marriage with Joanna, attracted not only by the wealth of the Castilian crown, but his recent memories of the lady, her pathetic character and tragic beauty. Henry's complex character had a chivalrous aspect. His agents abroad, including John Still, were full of stories that Joanna was kept in a state of confinement by her father. So Henry refused to believe that Joanna was mad.

Ferdinand had soon remarried after Isabella's death to the beautiful niece of Louis XII of France, Germaine de Foix. True, he opposed his daughter's marriage to Henry, though he hypocritically wrote to Dr. de Puebla, his ambassador in London that he favoured it:

If my daughter is to marry, I shall never consent that she weds with anyone else than the King of England, my brother, and shall employ the greatest love and good will all my industry and endeavour to promote that. But you must know that the said Queen, my daughter, still carries about with her the corpse *(el cuerpo)* of King Philip her late husband. Before I arrived they could never persuade her to bury him, and since my arrival she does not wish the said corpse to be buried.[11]

Henry, after 1503, still hoped to beget more sons, and since Joanna had already given birth to several healthy children, there was every reason to suppose that she could bear more. Avarice and ambition warred in Henry's mind, and a desire to strengthen his hand against Ferdinand for whom his dislike was to turn to hate.

De Puebla wrote to King Ferdinand on 15 April 1507 that the English seemed to care little for her insanity, since he had assured them that it would not prevent her from bearing children.[12] Five months later, he was informing Ferdinand that Henry and his Council desired extremely that the marriage should be concluded 'even if worse things should be said of her madness'. Catherine of Aragon wrote to her father favouring the marriage, thinking it might help her complicated relations with her father.

By 1506 her financial situation was becoming ever more precarious. It seemed unlikely that she would marry Harry now the Prince of Wales, and King Henry had other suitors in mind for his son. The 29 of June 1506 had been chosen as their wedding day, but it passed, and Ferdinand and Henry vied with one another how meanly they would treat her. Occasionally Henry would send her money, on one occasion £200, and smaller amounts, but the princess was constantly in debt and often there was no money for her servants' wages.

De Puebla's admiration for Henry VII was shared by many foreign ambassadors, particularly by the Milanese Raimondi de Raimondi de Sancini, who wrote on 8 September 1497 to Ludovico Sforza, Duke of Milan:

> In many things I know the King here to be most wise, but above all, because he is most thoroughly acquainted with the affairs of Italy, and receives especial information of every event. He is no less conversant with your own personal attributes and those of your duchy than the King of France, and when the King of France went into Italy the King of England sent with him a herald of his called Richmond, a wise man, who saw everything until the King's return.

The king was affable enough to foreigners and enjoyed himself with Sancini. A Florentine observer reported in 1496 that Henry was more feared than loved because of his avarice. Both Sancini and Trevisano, the Venetian envoy, bear witness to the state kept by the king and praised his clemency and ability to maintain good order. Sancini, writing on 26 January 1499, refers to Henry VII in the midst of all the turmoil 'like one standing at the top of a tower looking on what is passing in the plain'.

Henry was careful to keep on friendly terms with the duke of Milan. In December 1490 he wrote him:

> that he has learnt with much regret the seizure of some of your merchants together with their merchandise, on the Rhine, by the Count Palatine and the Margrave of Baden ... for we have not forgotten that last year when your Ambassador Francesco Pagnano was here we ... received all Milanese merchants under our safe conduct, so that they might safely and freely, like other foreign merchants, trade in this realm.

On 17 May 1499 we find Sancini writing to Ludovico Sforza: 'The King of England attends to nothing but amusements and to enjoying the infinite treasure which he has already amassed, and which he constantly augments.' This infers that Henry sometimes enjoyed himself and was not always perusing his account book. To the Borgia Pope Alexander VI, he commiserated on 12 January 1494 on learning of the enormous slaughter inflicted in Dalmatia and Croatia by the Turks, and the great danger, in which that country and every neighbouring province, especially Italy, is placed.

Pedro de Ayala, the able Spanish diplomat, wrote that the envy of the English was diabolical when the king expressed his greatest desire was to employ foreigners in his service. 'He likes to be much spoken of, and to be highly appreciated by the whole world. He fails in this because he is not a great King.' Ayala is incorrect when he says that Henry spent all his time he was not in Council in dealing with his accounts.

In his last years Henry was much with his mother, being greatly influenced by her. She only survived him a few months.

Herman Duque de Estrada (despite his proud title he was not an aristocrat) thought that Henry was devoted to his surviving son Henry, the heir to the throne. He wrote in 1504:

> Certainly there could be no better school in the world than the society of such a father as Henry VII. He is so wise and attentive to everything; nothing escapes his attention.

It is at least doubtful whether his opinion represented the truth, since the future Henry VIII resembled his maternal grandfather Edward IV in appearance and character much closer than his own father Henry Tudor. Nor did Henry VII prepare his son for kingship. Henry in boyhood and later as a young king was an attractive character, mostly extrovert, excelling in sports, high-spirited, daring, enjoying excellent health, and clever too. He composed a Latin speech for the benefit of the Dutch scholar Erasmus when he visited Eltham. One could not foresee the giant egotism nor the brutality of later years. One suspects that Henry VII, although an affectionate father to his children, may have been jealous of his surviving son knowing that he was ageing and that the boy had to succeed him. There are indications that young Henry was more intimate with his Yorkist mother.

XII HENRY AND HIS CONTEMPORARIES

Thomas More's early career began during Henry VII's reign, for he was born in 1478 and would have been seven on the king's succession in 1485. The great lawyer is the only author to give a detailed description of the murders of the princes in the Tower. Sir James Tyrell, governor of the fortress of Guisnes and his servant Dighton were both in the Tower in 1502 awaiting execution accused of high treason for aiding Edmund de La Pole, earl of Suffolk,[1] the rebel, supported by the Emperor Maximilian. After their conviction, they both confessed the manner of the princes' death, a confession contested by many supporters of Richard III. They question why Tyrell and his servant should confess to this crime when about to be executed for another crime. However, there was every reason for Tyrell to make a confession and seek absolution on the eve of death. There are inaccuracies in More's story of Sir James Tyrell being sent by Richard III from Warwick with orders to Sir Robert Brackenbury, governor of the Tower in 1483, to surrender the keys of the Tower to him for 'one night'. Thomas More, however, had already related that Richard ordered his servant John Green to tell Brackenbury to commit the murders, but, a man of honour, he had refused. According to More, Tyrell planned that the princes should be smothered, and appointed Miles Forest, one of their jailers, and John Dighton for this purpose.

Polydore Vergil, writing for Henry VII, corroborates More's account, though refraining from giving any details of the crime. Thomas, son of Sir John More, a judge of the King's Bench, had the finest legal mind in Europe. He was highly experienced in weighing and sifting evidence. A man of outstanding eminence and integrity, it is impossible to conceive that he would fabricate false evidence or attempt to deceive others. Yet there exists no absolute proof that his account is correct.

One contemporary Robert Fabyan, a London draper, almost the exact age of Richard III, a shrewd observer of the events of 1483, but writing some twenty-five years later, remarks:

Had Richard suffered the children to have prospered he would have been lauded over all whereas now his fame is darked and dishonoured as far as he is known.

There died during the autumn of 1500 one of King Henry's best friends, Cardinal Morton, one of the principal architects of foreign policy, but much criticized for his conduct in domestic affairs. Yet he had been to some extent responsible for the new unity and stability of the Tudor dynasty.[2] He has been unfairly said to have invented the policy known as 'Morton's Fork', a means of collecting new revenues for the king, but another counsellor Bishop Fox may be held responsible. Bacon describes the Archbishop Morton as a wise man but in his nature 'harsh and haughty'. Morton took a strong liking for the young page Thomas More and predicted his greatness in the future. He would exclaim to the lords dining with him at Lambeth Palace: 'This child here wayting at the table, whosoever shall live to see it, will proue a mervailous man.' Thomas More, a Londoner born in Milk Street in the ward of Cripplegate, would later praise his mentor for his great experience 'the verye mother and maistres of wisdom'. A great builder, Cardinal Morton used his church revenues to build parts of Lambeth Palace and the bell tower in Canterbury Cathedral.

John Fisher whose early career was much helped by the king's mother, the countess of Derby, was a friend of Thomas More and Erasmus, the humanist and Dutch scholar. Fisher, later bishop of Rochester, related that he first met the Lady Margaret when he dined with her in 1495 and their friendship became intimate and lasting. She was his patroness as the most influential figure in the University of Cambridge. She chose Fisher as her director to hear her confessions and to guide her life. Fisher was an outspoken man of great courage and as a zealous Roman Catholic was to defy his patroness's grandson later in his career and oppose Henry VIII's divorce. When two nunneries tried to suppress the foundation of St. John's College, Cambridge, Fisher prevented them from achieving it.

Cardinal Thomas Wolsey, Henry VIII's magnificent minister, began his career as a chaplain to his father, who certainly appreciated his ability. He had been sent on a diplomatic mission to James IV of Scotland and on another mission to Flanders when negotiations for a possible marriage between Mary, youngest daughter of Henry VII, and Archduke Charles took place.

The king never had a more faithful friend than Giles Daubeny, who began his military career serving Edward IV. He had been knighted in 1478 and two years later became Sheriff of Somerset and Dorset. After involvement in Buckingham's rebellion, he was attainted but fled abroad to join Henry Tudor. After fighting at Bosworth he became Captain of Calais and created a baron. He occupied high positions of trust, such as Chamberlain of the Household (1495) when he was close to the king and frequently attended meetings of the Council. He played an important part in suppressing the Cornish rising at Blackheath. His one failure was to omit accounting for some money when Captain of Calais for which he was fined £2,000 by King Henry.[3] Bernard André describes Daubeny as '*Vir bonus, prudens, justus, probus et omnibus dilectus*' (a good man, prudent, just, honest and beloved by everybody). He died in 1508, to be buried in St. Paul's Chapel, Westminster Abbey, with his family.

The most important patron of humanistic learning in the late fifteenth was Henry VII, and he did not confine his patronage to English scholars, for he also employed foreign humanists. He was not learned, but he appreciated learning.

Thomas Linacre was of All Souls, Oxford, travelled in Italy in 1485-6, was deeply interested in medicine and taught Greek after his return to Oxford in 1492. Nine years later, he was appointed tutor to Prince Arthur, having already established himself as physician to his father. During the reign of Henry's son he founded the College of Physicians in 1518, and established two lectureships in medicine at Merton College, Oxford, and another at St. Johns College, Cambridge. Another scholar to breathe the spirit of the Italian Renaissance was John Colet, son of a Lord Mayor of London, who travelled to Florence and Bologna. Returning to Oxford, he became famous for his expositions to *Romans* and the *Corinthians*.

Thomas More, aged twenty-three, was much influenced by Colet, and even considered entering the priesthood. In 1504, however, he was elected to parliament and may have prejudiced his career by courageously resisting Henry VII's financial transactions.

The spirit of the Italian Renaissance pervaded Henry's court. Fond of employing foreigners despite English prejudice he employed many Italians in his service. Giovanni Gigli, formerly a papal collector, was appointed diplomatic agent in Rome, while his nephew Silvestro served as the king's master of ceremonies and later in 1499 as ambassador in Rome. Both Giovanni and Silvestro became bishops of Worcester. Another Italian, Adrian de Castello,was appointed bishop of Hereford in 1502 and after two years bishop of Bath and Wells.[4] Henry had his own Latin secretary, Pietro Cormeliano, born in Brescia in 1451. He received a crown pension, probably obtained as a reward for writing a poem celebrating the birth of Prince Arthur in September 1486.[5] A letter exists in his beautiful handwriting written in Latin in which Henry expresses considerable affection for Joanna of Castile archduchess of Austria and Burgundy. The letter was written on 8 April 1497, in Sheen and signed Henricus.

The king possessed artistic taste and encouraged Flemish and Italian artists to come to London, sending to Italy for Italian furniture, cloth of gold and damask. Rich church vestments were embroidered for him in Florence. The Florentine sculptor Pietro Torrigiano was highly regarded by the king and was later to work on tombs of Henry and his queen and Lady Margaret Beaufort, works of surpassing merit. As already mentioned, the king enjoyed his intimate relations with the dukes of Milan, Ferrara and Urbino. He conferred the high honour of the Order of the Garter on the latter prince.

XIII HENRY'S INTERESTS AND PASTIMES

Henry VII was much attached to architecture and to building. His favourite palace was Sheen in Surrey named after an old Saxon word for a beauty spot, but an early palace at Sheen was closely associated with the medieval King Richard II, who destroyed it after the death of his queen, Anne of Bohemia. He could no longer bear to live there, having too many happy memories.

Henry had planned to spend Christmas 1487 at Sheen, but on the night of 24 December, while he, his queen and family were in residence, a fire destroyed valuable furniture, jewels and plate.[1] The whole building was ruined. In its place over three years later, the king built a royal palace in the Gothic style. The Privy Lodgings where the royal family lived when in residence were decorated with fourteen turrets. To climb to the tower it was necessary to ascend one hundred and twenty steps. As Sheen now had unfortunate memories for the king, he decided to rename it Richmond Palace in 1503, giving it the name of his title the earl of Richmond, the Yorkshire honour he had held before Bosworth. With its lovely view of the silvery Thames, Henry was even more attached to Richmond Palace and was to die there in April 1509. Unfortunately, the only original part remaining is the old palace gatehouse with the king's arms.

Elizabeth of York, when alive, had been especially fond of Greenwich Palace. Margaret of Anjou had named the palace 'Placentia', but Henry VII changed its name to Greenwich. He refaced the building with red brick. Prince Henry, the king's younger son, had been born there in 1491 and Prince Edmond in 1499. Another palace much liked by the king was Eltham because the hunting in its park and neighbourhood had many advantages. It was beloved by medieval kings, including Henry IV. With its moat and Great Hall, it possessed much beauty. Woodstock in Oxfordshire was often visited by Henry. At Windsor Castle, the king completed work to St. George's Chapel, built by Edward IV. He also rebuilt Baynard's Castle on the banks of the Thames.

When in London to attend his parliaments, Henry lived in the Palace of Westminster where he would sleep in Henry III's painted chamber. Far the most important and noblest of his buildings was the Henry VII Chapel, which replaced the former Lady Chapel. With its fan-vaulted roof, it delights the many people who visit it today as it has delighted our ancestors for nearly five centuries. Begun during January 1503, a month before the death of Henry's queen and intended as a shrine for the murdered Henry VI, the king's intention was never realized. The relics of the holy King Henry VI were never removed to Westminster. Taken from Chelsea to Windsor, Richard III had had Henry VI reburied to the right of the high altar in St. George's Chapel. Henry VII wanted his revered forebear canonized, but six years later, there were still delays to this momentous step. Abbot John Islip, on very friendly terms with Henry VII, laid the foundation stone on 24 January and the king bound the abbot and convent of Westminster to contribute £500 to the cost of the building. Sir Reginald Bray, among many other accomplishments a keen architect, did much work on the design of the chapel, but he died on 5 April 1503, a few months after the first foundation stone had been laid. The Abbey took sixteen years to complete, and Henry was never to see that day.

The Abbot Islip, born in the village of that name in Oxfordshire, occasionally had King Henry to dine with him at the Manor of Cheyneygates (the name is derived from the French word chêne, an oak). Henry was very fond of the marrow-bone puddings prepared by the Abbot's excellent cook. On Friday 11 June when Henry dined with Islip, there would naturally be no meat served, but presumably fish. We know that the wine and strawberries together cost 3s. 8d. and a barrel of ale 2s. Islip's household accounts among the Abbey muniments reveal that Islip and the king had many discussions in which they mentioned the new chapel being planned. From 1502 onwards, Henry would give the abbot an annual present of two tuns of wine. He created Islip a Privy Councillor, and he subsequently became treasurer or paymaster for the Henry VII Chapel. The total expenses for the building amounted to £14,000 and the king is said to have sent Islip £5,000 ten days before his death. It is a marvel of Gothic architecture, and the stone used for the chapel came from Huddlestone quarry in Yorkshire. Francis Bond wrote of it with its exquisite and colourful stalls of the Knights of the Bath:

> It is far in advance of anything of contemporary date in England or France, or Italy or Spain. It shows us Gothic architecture not sinking into senile decay, as some have idly taught, but bursting forth phoenix-like, into new life, instinct with the freshness and originality of youth.

Henry is altogether a more human character than he is usually depicted by historians. For instance, from his household accounts, we learn that he kept many jesters at his court, surely a medieval taste. Perhaps the so-called 'foolyshe duc de Lancaster' is the best known. To Diego, his Spanish jester, Henry once presented a horse with a saddle and bridle. Henry liked to be amused, could be witty enough on occasions, and possessed a gift for repartee. The antics of jugglers and clowns gave him rich amusement. When a pretty young girl danced before him, he rewarded her liberally, hardly the action of a man dubbed always mean.[2] He was not averse to dice or games[3] of chance, and was fond of cards. A moderate gambler, he sometimes lost, but we are not told when he won. There are numerous payments to morris dancers, to play-actors, 'to a tumbler upon the rope', 'to Ringeley Abbot of Misrule'. He was keen to reward musicians, like 'the Welsh harper' 6s. 8d. or 'to Walt the luter that played the lute'. To my Lady Mary (almost certainly Henry's younger daughter), he paid 13s. 4d. for a lute and for a pair of organs £30. To a Spanish musician, he gave on one occasion £10 and an Italian poet £20.

For rare animals such as lions, leopards, wild cats and foreign birds, he had a real fancy and many fellow rulers knowing this gave him various animals, but he was willing to pay a high price for them. For a common nightingale he once paid one pound.

It would be surprising if Henry was not religious with a mother so addicted to good works. He was indeed a highly orthodox Roman Catholic, enjoying tactful and respectful relations with the contemporary popes. Henry possessed the conventional religious beliefs and superstitions of his era.[4] He could be generous in his almsgiving, and was meticulous in his religious observances and his respect for relics. He was no more merciful to heretics than other strict Roman Catholics such as Thomas More, but we must not apply to him the standards of today. During the 24 years of his reign, Henry VII, intolerant of heresy, had 11 heretics burnt to death at the stake, while his son later had 80 heretics during his reign suffering a similar fate. On one occasion Henry VII is said to have made a heretic retract, paying him 6s. 8d., only to allow the man to be burnt at the stake when he should have been spared. On 24 April 1494, a woman almost aged eighty was burnt at the stake. 'And never would she turne him the said heresys for noon exhortacion, but in the said heronyous opyyions died'.[5]

There was a great deal of immorality in the Church in Henry's time, among priests and monks, and the king did his utmost to prevent it. In his early reign, Cardinal Morton had been told to visit monasteries and religious houses, and to make reforms, if necessary. Two of the worst dioceses were the Welsh diocese of Bangor and St. David's where 80 celibate priests kept mistresses while paying lipservice to the church. The result was that some friars were removed from office owing to misconduct.

Although not erudite, he was studious, spending considerable money on manuscripts and printed books. He is said to have given William Caxton, so associated with Westminster, the French text of *The Book of Fayttes of Armes and of Chivalrie* (published in London in 1490) for translation and printing. To the printer Pryson, he gave an advance of £10 to publish a mass book. Henry possessed copies of Froissart, being able to read them in the original French. He paid as much as £25 to a Frenchman for a book, and to somebody called Anthony Verard, he gave six pounds for two books, entitled 'The Gardyn of Health'. The king loved jewellery, spending £100,000 on it for 14 years from 1491-1505, seemingly an extravagance, but he probably looked upon it as a solid investment.

Though Henry's relations with his mother continued warm and loving to the end, he occasionally disagreed with her. He did not approve of her sister Cecily's second marriage to Thomas Kymber in 1503, probably because he was of the opinion that Kymber was not suitable as a husband for a daughter of Edward IV. The Lady Margaret, however, supported her and had her to stay at her home in Northamptonshire, Collyweston on the river Welland. She continued her good works, maintaining at Hatfield twelve poor men and women whom she often visited, ministering to them with her own hands when they were ill. She concerned herself wholeheartedly in promoting education and at Wimborne where the duke and duchess of Somerset were buried, she endowed a chantry of one priest. Henry was influenced by her in many ways, particularly when making episcopal appointments, for a number of livings were in her gift.

Margaret during her entire life had thought first of 'my own sweet and most dear king and all my worldly joy'. There is evidence that in 1501, eight years before his death, Henry feared that his eyesight was failing him and that he even might become blind. Writing to her in July,[6] he refers to the Statute of Mortmain, having agreed to dispense with the statute so as to allow her to proceed with one of her foundations at Cambridge:

All of which things according to your desire and pleasure, I have, with all my heart and good will given and granted you; and my dame, not only in this but in all other things that I know should be to your honour and pleasure, and weal of your soul, I shall be glad to please you as your heart can desire it, and I know well, that I am as much bounden to do, as any creature living for the great and singular motherly love and affection that it hath pleased you at all times to bear me.

He apologizes to her that he writes to her so seldom, for he confesses 'my sight is nothing so perfect as it has been...' This letter, which also mentions her confessor and close friend John Fisher, was written at Greenwich.

During the last two years of his life, it was not only his eyesight that was failing him. He was often very ill, of a 'quinsy' during the spring of 1507. Then it was feared he would die again in July 1508 when he had to endure a bout of consumption.

Henry realized the importance of trade with The Netherlands and several clauses in what was called the *intercursus malus* by the Flemings, a commercial treaty signed in 1506, worked greatly to the advantage of English merchants. Owing, however, to the death of the Archduke Philip during late September 1506, the commercial treaty was never ratified. Henry also was bent on improving the trading prospects of the English merchants in the Baltic and Scandinavia to the detriment of the powerful Hanseatic League of German merchants in the Baltic ports. However, the king's policy only had limited success.[7]

Towards the end of the reign of Henry VII, Dr. de Puebla, the Spanish ambassador, was often ill and was becoming old and tired. His salary was often in arrears, so that he sometimes lived at court to save expense. Indeed, de Puebla had been compelled to sell the small properties he owned in Spain to pay his creditors. Meanwhile, he bore the incessant complaints of Princess Catherine with any composure he could muster, especially when Catherine wrote to Ferdinand, her father, that the Spanish ambassador told nothing but lies about her. In reality, though the position was very intricate, de Puebla constantly pleaded her cause with both Henry and Ferdinand.

Ferdinand's relations with Henry had now become very strained; and fearing that they would develop into something even worse, decided to send his daughter formal credentials as his ambassador[8] and to communicate directly with Henry. Catherine now revealed unexpected ability in her interviews with Henry, learning to weigh men and events, and such qualities that are invaluable in diplomacy, patience and tact. Her father had told her that the friendship of Spain and England depended on her marriage to Henry Prince of Wales. At all costs that must be achieved.

Ferdinand could not have chosen a more unsuitable special ambassador to represent him at Henry's court than Don Guiterre Gomez de Fuensalida (now Governor of Membrilla). True, he came of an ancient family from Castile, and he had given good service at Maximilian's and Philip's court, but he was too outspoken, lacked tact, subtlety, and the ability to acquire the confidence of the rulers of the countries in which he was employed. Ayala, who knew King Henry well, would have been a better choice. However, Fuensalida from the first did not have any 'rapport' with the King of England, who in his last years was becoming increasingly sensitive to slights and irascible. Fuensalida reached London on 22 February 1508, having been told by King Ferdinand to consult with de Puebla, who remarried in England. Fuensalida, however, shared Ayala's opinion of de Puebla, and consulted him reluctantly. At their first interview Henry assured the ambassador that he loved Catherine like his own daughter and would prefer her for his son to any lady in Christendom. Of course, he had had many better offers.

When he met the Council a few days later, Richard Fox, Nicholas West, the earl of Surrey and others, Fuensalida said that he had come to pay the final instalment of Princess Catherine's dowry and to ensure that the marriage treaty should follow. When Fox requested the ambassador to tell him how the 65,000 crowns owing would be paid, Fuensalida said at once. There were unpleasant exchanges about the jewels and plate Catherine had brought with her to England during October 1501, Fuensalida declaring in a loud voice that if the Princess had had to pay her debts by realizing some of the jewels and plate originally worth 35,000 crowns, it was owing to Henry's meanness. The Council made a counter-charge that Ferdinand's behaviour had been unkingly. After much bluster and complaints on Fuensalida's part, the Council firmly declared that they would accept no part of Catherine's jewellery or plate as payment for her dowry. In his despatches to Ferdinand, Fuensalida made many references to Catherine's privations.

In his dilemma, Fuensalida felt obliged at last to ask de Puebla for his advice. That experienced envoy told his colleague that the English would have to take the jewels and plate (heavily depleted in value) unless they intended to repudiate the treaty. He advised Fuensalida to wait until the east winds subsided before seeing the king again. He was likely to be easier to negotiate with. De Puebla wanted to have a talk with Henry to smooth matters over, but Fuensalida haughtily rebuffed him. Meanwhile Ferdinand had sent a draft for 10,000 ducats, which made up in value for the fall in value of the plate.

Owing to de Puebla, Fuensalida was admitted to another interview with King Henry at Greenwich. The discussion was concerned mostly with the King of England's desire to marry Joanna of Castile, Ferdinand's daughter. He had now been given instructions by Ferdinand to encourage Henry with his plans to marry Joanna, but the ambassador was of the opinion that Joanna could never marry anybody. Henry, however, asked him pointedly:

Tell me, Ambassador, is the Queen (of Castile) such as they say she is? If what they say is true, God defend that I should marry her for three kingdoms such as hers, but there are those who say it is your King who keeps her shut up and spreads this rumour about her. Indeed I have had reports from Spain that she listens and replies rationally and seems quite normal. when I saw her two years ago, her husband and some of his Council were declaring that she was mad, but at that time I saw her speak and act rationally and with great grace and dignity.[9]

The king still thought her sane... Fuensalida did not know what to say, merely muttering that whatever the state of mind the queen was, surely the king was too old to think of marriage. He was over fifty; hardly a tactful remark for a Spanish envoy.

Henry was anxious that his youngest daughter Mary should marry Charles of Gwent, the son of Philip the Handsome, now deceased, and grandson of the Emperor Maximilian, a brilliant marriage for Mary Tudor since Charles was both powerful and wealthy, though aged fourteen. Instead of filling Henry's mind with hopes that Ferdinand would support the marriage, Fuensalida told the king that Ferdinand had no real intention of sanctioning the marriage. He had shown resentment when a treaty for the marriage had been signed on 21 December 1507, accompanied by a Treaty of Mutual Alliance between Charles (later Emperor Charles V) and Henry. Mary shared her father's eagerness for the match. She impressed Erasmus, who wrote:

> O thrice and four times happy our illustrious Prince, who is to have such a bride! Nature never made anyone more beautiful; and she excels in goodness and wisdom.[10]

There were constant delays to the marriage and eventually it never took place. When forced into a marriage with the old roué Louis XII of France early in her brother Henry VIII's reign, Mary made him promise that in the event of Louis's death she should be allowed to marry Charles Brandon, created duke of Suffolk.

Catherine of Aragon might blame her father-in-law King Henry for keeping her in financial straits, but her own behaviour from 1506 onwards was far from blameless. Doña Elvira, her domineering duenna, had returned to Spain in 1505, but she unfortunately allowed her confessor Fray Diego Fernandez, appointed in 1506, to acquire far too great an influence over her. There seems some justification for Fuensalida describing this friar, now Catherine's chancellor, as 'a pestiferous person' when writing to his master King Ferdinand. 'He was light, haughty and licentious to an extreme degree. He gained her confidence and affection.'

Fuensalida now regretted his bitter criticism of Henry VII. He was on bad terms with the Princess of Wales, having witnessed too much scandal prevailing in her household. 'May God forgive me,' he wrote to King Ferdinand, 'but now that I know so well the affairs of the princess's household, I acquit the King of England of a great portion of the blame which I hitherto gave him.'[11]

Catherine was now aged over twenty, having been born in 1485, and she became even more hostile to Fuensalida than she had been to de Puebla. It is possible that Fray Diego Fernandez had a physical affair with the princess, for she was so besotted with him.

Throughout the affair, Henry behaved with considerable forbearance. On one occasion, the king expressed a wish that Catherine should go to visit him at Richmond, but the princess refused, influenced by Diego Fernandez. On the following day, she came to Richmond attended by only three of her women, the friar, and two servants. Henry was naturally offended by her behaviour, and for three weeks took no notice of Catherine, omitting to inquire about her health when she fell ill. The ambassador wrote that the princess had sold some gold plate for 200 ducats, used mainly for Diego Fernandez's expenses.[12] She blamed Francesca de Carceres, the most vivacious of her women, as the source of Fuensalida's information. The household of the princess seethed with intrigue and discontent.

Fuensalida, although he did not lack either courage or pertinacity, failed completely as a negotiator. Bishop Fox, who was an expert in this field, on one occasion told him: 'You know, Ambassador, he is a bad cook who spoils good food with unpalatable sauce. Most ambassadors try to present things as pleasantly as possible, and keep the good will of him to whom they are sent.' He continued to interrupt and antagonize King Henry. When Henry remarked that for many years Ferdinand had not a 100,000 crowns to pay for his daughter's dowry, the ambassador could not refrain from saying:

> Señor, the King, my master, is equal in fame and glory and power to any prince in Christendom. He does not lock away his gold in chests, but pays it to the brave soldiers at whose head he has always been and will always be victorious.

– an insolence that so stung the king that for some time he refused Fuensalida an interview.

Throughout her adversity, Catherine had always clung to the hope that she would marry Henry Prince of Wales, although they remained faint while Henry VII remained alive. Fuensalida on his side had abandoned hope that Catherine would ever wed Henry and planned her return to Spain. He was of the opinion that the prince was in complete subjection to his father and grandmother and had very little will of his own, being surrounded by tutors and companions chosen by his father. True, he was extremely handsome and excelled in horsemanship. He had red-gold hair, and a massive body.

William Warham, who had shown considerable ability as a diplomat and enjoyed Henry VII's confidence, was appointed Archbishop of Canterbury in 1503 and during the following year chancellor on 21 January, retaining the office until the end of 1515 when Henry VIII was on the throne.

The old king (considered so in that age) towards the end of his life had lost his good looks, his complexion was sallow, his teeth black and decayed, and his hair was thinning.

Henry was still determined to oppose the power of the established City companies, especially the Mercers, one of the older, richer companies, whose origin lay before the late twelfth century. Its headquarters were by Cheapside and Ironmonger Lane. In early Tudor times, it was known as 'Compeny', or the 'Mystere of Mercers', or 'craft of the City', guild or fellowship.[13] In the late fifteenth century it was composed of other companies including the merchant adventurers and their business interests concerned the export of cloth and wool. The king's favourite was the merchant taylors – a new guild – and he resorted to outright interference in City elections. Opposed to Henry was Thomas More, the leading light in the Mercers, now a freeman and as an able lawyer determined to defend its interests when Henry became a menace threatening to levy a new tax upon cloth exports. This policy was to alienate many people. Thomas More detested his financial transactions and considered him tyrannical.

There are many portraits of Henry VII painted during his lifetime, the well-known portrait in oil when the king was aged forty-eight in 1505 by Michel Sittow,[14] commissioned by the Emperor Maximilian I to be sent to Margaret of Savoy, one of his possible brides. Another portrait painted in his lifetime about 1500 was known to be included in the inventory of Henry VIII. Torrigiano made a superb bust of Henry about 1508-9, the best depiction now existing. The head of the tomb effigy on Henry's tomb in Westminster by the same Florentine artist was done between 1512-1519. There is an altar piece at Windsor showing Henry, his queen and their offspring adoring St. George made about 1505-9, certainly during his lifetime, but it cannot be described as a portrait.

There is an interesting sketch of Henry of Richmond when young by Jacques Leboucq de Valenciennes, Hainault Herald in the Library of Arras, probably dating from 1559-1560. No original portrait of Queen

Elizabeth of York exists. There is a picture in the National Portrait Gallery, by an unknown artist probably dating from the sixteenth century.

The transept window of Great Malvern Priory Church is well worth a visit, for it has interesting pictures of King Henry VII, Queen Elizabeth of York, Prince Arthur and Sir Reginald Bray. The window is of considerable beauty, an exquisite specimen of fifteenth century English stained glass. The north transept window was the royal gift of Henry VII, almost certainly executed by the glaziers of Westminster in 1501. King Henry and Prince Arthur are in perfect condition, but Elizabeth of York over the years has been ruined. Arthur Prince of Wales is dressed in armour, and kneels on a green cushion in front of a desk, and the king is in a very similar setting. This is known as the Magnificat window.

XIV HENRY'S RAPACITY

There is considerable evidence that Henry VII became increasingly rapacious during the last six years of his life, after the death of his queen, though one eminent historian,[1] Professor G.R. Elton, disputes it. He was always eager for money, loving it during his reign, as one constantly lacking it during his fourteen years of exile, prior to becoming king. He was no miser, however, for he spent money freely where it was expedient for him to do so. It would be fair to say that he saved and extorted money in the interests of the Crown rather than for himself. Solvency deeply concerned him, for it was the basis of sound government. For ten years he pursued a vigorous policy for the enlargement of his prerogative rights, and this did not involve abuses in the law. Investigating commissions were organized to discover the king's rights in the lands of tenants-in-chief.

From 1500 onwards a Committee of the Council, known as the King's Council, learned in the law, sat regularly as a tribunal under the presidency of the Chancellor of the Duchy of Lancaster. While Sir Reginald Bray held office, his actions were never questioned, but it was otherwise with Sir Richard Empson. The Council Learned decided cases brought by the Crown, and was concerned with offences committed in office, especially by sheriffs. Both sheriffs and bishops were fined for letting prisoners escape. The Council Learned was a typical Tudor court, a royal tribunal rather than a regular court of the realm. Its contemporaries attacked it for its insistence on reviving ancient laws long since fallen into abeyance.

It was unfortunate for the king's ultimate reputation for rapacity and extortion that he employed Edmund Dudley and Richard Empson as his agents in extracting money from his subjects. They were both to become deeply unpopular, even hated by most people, accused of packing juries, of making false accusations to extract money by compositions, of mixing accusations under expired statutes with more proper proceedings and attacking people that were dead through their executors.

The date of Edmund Dudley's alleged birth, 1462, is probably incorrect, but it is very likely that he studied law at Gray's Inn. The training of a student was very prolonged, for it usually lasted seven or eight years. It was in the Star Chamber that Dudley acquired most of his experience, for it is known that he never held high office in the law courts. Before rising to the position of Speaker of the House of Commons in 1504, Dudley held the legal office of Under-Sheriff of London for five years. It was his knowledge of commercial affairs that induced Henry VII to make him a valuable councillor. He is recorded to have made an appearance on the Learned Council during a session in the Star Chamber to decide the disputes between the merchant adventurers and merchant Staples concerning the creation of a free mart in Calais. Miss D.M. Brodie has done much detailed research on Henry VII's councillor.[2] He was the grandson of the Lancastrian supporter John Lord Dudley, who was imprisoned together with Henry VI after the Battle of St. Albans (1455). Edmund Dudley's grandson was the famous Robert Dudley, created earl of Leicester by Henry VII's granddaughter, Elizabeth I.

Francis Bacon wrote of King Henry 'that he did not care how cunning those were that he did employ; for he thought himself to have the master-reach'.[3] Bacon relates 'a merry tale' about Henry's pet monkey, which was encouraged by one of his chamber to destroy one of his principal notebooks in which he confided his thoughts 'whereat the court, which liked not those pensive accounts, was almost tickled with sport'.[4] He writes of Henry: 'of nature assuredly he coveted to accumulate treasures and was a little poor in admiring riches'.

There is little doubt that the king, especially in his last six years, abused his royal powers. To fill his coffers he would fine his nobles and wealthy citizens with the utmost ruthlessness. Empson and Dudley were but his instruments. He was hardly scrupulous 'in crushing treasure out of his subjects' purses, by forfeiture under penal laws'. He would fine lord mayors and aldermen for their alleged offences whilst holding office, and he imposed heavy fines on Sir William Capell and Thomas Kneysworth for various misdemeanours.

From Dudley's account book, we know that he collected £65,361 for the king during 1506-7. Empson and Dudley caused much resentment because they filled their own pockets and relied on professional informers or promoters as they were named. The worst offender was John Baptist Brimaldi, who Dudley accused in his will of knowing everything. He wrote 'all thinges consideryd (he) mought have dwelt with me better than he dyde'.

Dudley held no brief for tyranny and probably does not deserve all the censure with which his name is usually associated. He wrote a book called *The Tree of Commonwealth* (1509), a manual written for the education of a prince rather than a political treatise. It should be judged as a medieval allegory, replete with medieval commonplaces, about the necessity of 'keeping troth'. However, it pays the highest regard to the feudal nobility

107

as being the chivalry of the realm. He explains that he could not decide any law suit himself, but must act through deputies and obey where possible ancient procedure. *The Tree of Commonwealth*[5] is the first English book to emphasize that the growing power of councillors and officials – today we might call them bureaucrats – was likely to become as formidable a menace to the pure administration of justice as had formerly been the influence of a great nobleman. Since he feared social turmoil, Dudley was keen to emphasize the responsibilities of kingship for the impartial administration of justice. Dudley was at least loyal to the last to Henry VII, who was:

> in manner without faulte, saving only that he was inclined to set his felicity too much on world treasure and consequently failed to gain that popular affection, so often wasted on more superficial characters.

He described himself as one who bore 'a hartie good will and love towards the prosperous estate of my naturall countrie'.

Polydore Vergil is the chief contemporary writer critical of Henry after 1504. He is of the opinion that his character sadly deteriorated. He accuses Empson and Dudley of malpractices.

Richard Empson was of humble birth, the son of a sieve-maker. Both he and Dudley were arrested very early in Henry VIII's reign by the new King's or Council's order and imprisoned in the Tower. Aware of how deeply they were hated by the people, Henry wanting to gain a cheap popularity had them accused of constructive treason – a fictitious charge.[6] True, they were ruthless agents of his father's policy, harsh and often corrupt, in reality scapegoats for the oppressive acts of the last years.

Whilst awaiting trial in the Tower, Dudley made a confession to Bishop Fox, Keeper of the Privy Seal, and to Sir Thomas Lovell, Chancellor of the Exchequer. He also signed a petition[7] to these ministers. It included as many as eighty-four cases of unjust exactions for which he considered the executors of Henry VII's will should make restitution. Typical examples are these:

(1) Item one Haslewood was kept long in prison and paid a great sum of money upon a light ground.
(2) Item one Catesby of Northampton was in a manner undone upon a light surmise.
(3) Item the earl of Northumberland was bound to the king in many great sums, howbeit the king's mind was to have payment of £2,000 and no more, as his grace showed me, yet that was too much for ought that was known.

(4)   Item a poor gentleman of Kent called Roger Appleton paid 100 marks upon an untrue matter.

(5)   Item one Simmes a haberdasher without Ludgate paid and must pay £500 for light matters only upon a surmise of a lewd quean.

(6)   Item the king had the substance of Nicholas Nivesgoods, by reason of another man's obligation given unto his grace for his wife and creditors had nothing.

(7)   Item the Lord Abergeny had a very sore end, for any proof that was against him to my knowledge.

(8)   Item doctor Horsey was long in prison and paid £100 in my mind contrary to conscience.

(9)   Item one Windial a poor man in Devonshire lay long in prison and paid £100 upon a very small cause.

Edmund Dudley worded his petition in this manner:

The petition of Edward Dudley the most wretched and sorrowfull creature beinge a dead man by the Kinge's lawyers a prisoner in the Tower of London there abydeing life or death (To whom I never offended in treason or thinge licke to it to my knowledge as my sinfull soul be saved) ...

He mentions that in the late king's will special provision must be made to all persons wronged by his grace.

While Empson, Dudley and others were responsible for harsh deeds and miscarriages of justice, there is no doubt that Henry retained close executive power over their actions. Francis Bacon saw Empson's account book, and it is evident that every page contained the king's hand. A sixteenth century copy of the petition of Edmund Dudley survives, formerly discovered in a box of unlisted material of Plas Newdd papers, the property of the Marquis of Anglesea.

On 6 July 1510 Dudley was found guilty on a charge of constructive treason, and executed on 17 August. Empson, tried and sentenced at Northampton, met a similar fate.

Dudley's confession, written in prison shortly before execution, is sincere enough and he had no motive for mendacity. During the last year or so of his life, Henry expressed remorse for some of the excesses, perhaps as a genuinely religious man, knowing that he would soon have to answer for his deed to God. In his will[8] he was determined to set up a committee to investigate:

the circumstances if any person of what degree so ever he be, show by any complaint to our executors any wrong to have been done to him, by us, by our commandment, occasion or mean, or that we held any goods or lands which of right ought to appertain to him.

The king's flair for finance amounted almost to genius, and he was fortunate in his treasurers of the Chamber, Sir Thomas Lovell and John Heron, who succeeded Lovell in 1506 in this office, retaining the title for 18 years. He was destined to fulfill the role of a key figure in early Tudor administration, a civil servant rather than a minister. The care he took in keeping the account books of Henry VII can only be understood when one visits the Public Record Office now at Kew and an examination of the account books reveals how frequently they were scrutinized and initialled by the king. Lovell in his early reign, and subsequently Heron presented their chamber accounts 'to the King's highness', who took enormous interest in them. John Heron won golden opinions from Henry VII and Henry VIII, whose personal interest in the accounts and business of the Chamber was nothing like as keen as his father's. Heron was a man of great integrity, efficiency and honesty. Many Privy Seal writs exist ordering the payment of monies to John Heron, treasurer of the Chamber often of unspecified amounts, but all described as debts owed to the king.

Heron's chamber accounts were only audited by Henry VII, who himself personally handled many transactions, receiving cash.[9] Heron survived until 1524.

My lady the king's mother, her husband the earl of Derby and young Henry Lord of York (duke of York) all figure in the account books and other items concern the pages of the king's chamber, the king's porter and his trumpeter.[10]

Many of the bonds mentioned represented commercial actions by the king to Italian and English merchants for licences to export wool and import wines. Also for hire of the king's ships. Other bonds are more open to suspicion, those made for the release of criminals from prison, for the pardon of murderers and other felons, and for the pardons of rebels after the Cornish rebellion (1497). In one of the chamber books John Heron has a curious mention about certain persons who are not yet through with the king's name and 'his said grace hath a list of their names'.

Henry VII's reform of the currency, which was in a chaotic condition in the early years, was one of his wisest measures.[11] Debased, clipped and foreign coins were in circulation leading to much abuse. Bad Irish coinage was frequently used, so special steps were resorted to, to stop this. Those guilty of forging foreign and English coin were charged with high treason. An Act of Parliament (1504) set exacting standards. Gold coins were only valid if of full weight, while clipped coins must be refused and it was obligatory for new coins to be stamped with a circle round the edge to prevent clipping. The law concerning silver coins was not so rigid and light (though not clipped silver coins) could be accepted if containing the royal stamp. The clipping of coin was an offence punishable by death, and a case is recorded of a false coiner during 1505 being hung at Tyburn.[12] The king also reformed the standard weights and measures.

The Crown never became more despotic and powerful during the reign of the first Tudor. What weighed with Henry was to make his kingdom strong and powerful. There was a mass of industrial and agrarian legislation. Unlike modern government, he did not consider the happiness of his subjects.

The king's shrewdness in managing his income can be perceived at the beginning of his reign. From 1485-90 it averaged about £52,000, hardly sufficient to meet new expenses and pay back old debts, so he resorted to borrowing from bishops, from the City of London, from Italian merchants and from the Staplers. Henry was always ready to repay what he borrowed promptly. Seven years after ascending the throne, his royal accounts provided a surplus and by 1497 Henry began to save money in a large way. For the last five years of his life, his income had reached the huge amount of £142,000. His expenditure was high too – £138,000 – but much of this money was spent on jewels as an investment or paid out in loans. When he died, he left not only money in currency, but jewels, plate and bonds. It was a real balance, mentioned by tradition according to Francis Bacon, as £1,800,000 and more likely as the real amount by the Venetian ambassador as £1,300,000. It is important, however, to stress that Henry enriched himself, and also his country. By his extravagance and gross egotism, Henry VIII was to dissipate his father's fortune.

EPILOGUE

During the last year of Henry's life the League of Cambrai (1508) designed against Venice was signed by Ferdinand of Aragon, the Emperor Maximilian, Louis XII of France and Pope Julius II, but England was never a party to it. All these countries, however, were careful to maintain friendly relations with Henry, and the king because of his patience and skill was regarded in Europe with deep respect. Maximilian still hoped that Henry's youngest daughter Mary should marry his grandson the Archduke Charles (later Charles V), but it never became more than a proxy wedding. Henry was a very clever king. When he died a year later, the orientation of foreign policy he had worked for so laboriously was completely transformed. Of quite a different temperament, his successor Henry VIII loved military glory where his father sought for peace, only resorting to war with the greatest reluctance. France was the traditional enemy and young Henry's craving for martial glamour was popular with the English. He was not yet nineteen when he ascended the throne.

Henry VII was feared rather than loved, yet one of the strongest of our kings, decisive and what he minded he compassed as Bacon wrote. Where his granddaughter Elizabeth I, the greatest of our queens, resembled him was in her care for money and in her parsimony, but unlike him suffering from constant moods of irresolution and indecision. She possessed, above all, the supreme quality of inspiring her people. Who can read her magnificent speech at Tilbury before the Spanish Armada without emotion. There were many dramatic events during Henry VII's reign but in his reserved, undemonstrative character there were few signs of drama, a oneness with the people over whom he ruled.

During the later sixteenth century, England reached a greatness, only possible because of the seed sown by the first Tudor king, grasping the importance for trade of the early voyages of discovery of John and Sebastian Cabot and attracting learned men to his court, both Englishmen and foreigners.

King Henry VII was primarily a statesman and in this capacity he must be judged immensely hardworking, fortunate in the men who served him, such as Archbishop Morton, Reginald Bray and Richard Fox. A lesser man might well have succumbed to the Pretender Warbeck, accepted by many rulers in Europe and Scotland for a while, but Henry was made of sterner mettle. His supreme achievement was to found a dynasty, to become a despot and to leave an example of successful despotism to his son, a strong title as has been said, a great treasure, a subservient nobility, a dependent church and a submissive parliament. Yet this man with his many varied interests was regarded in his own age with a cold dislike or distaste by many, even hatred by some. His great work of consolidation, for he was no innovator, is insufficiently appreciated today. He was partly medieval in his outlook, one who possessed curious beliefs of dark superstition. He had been betrayed too often, hence there lurked in his character a natural suspicion and distrust of those around him and a secretiveness that increased with advancing age.

Just before his death Henry sent for his surviving son and told him to marry Catherine of Aragon, so long held in subjection, but now eagerly wanted by young Henry. Joanna of Castile, who had for several years attracted the old king, lived on, subjected to imprisonment or at least confinement, firstly by her own father and then her son Charles until 1555 at Tardesillas in Spain in the direst misery. Perhaps she was never really mad until towards the end of her life.

Francis Bacon was to write of King Henry: 'He had nothing in him of vainglory, but yet kept state and majesty to the height.' Abroad, his reputation and stature was even higher than at home. 'His good fortune,' wrote an Italian visitor ('an Italian Relation'):

> has been equal to his spirit, for he has never lost a battle. From the time of William the Conqueror, no King has reigned more peaceably than he has, his great prudence causing him to be universally feared.

When he engaged in battle – and it was a rare occasion – he always emerged the victor, at least financially.

So greatly was Henry esteemed by foreign statesmen that Cardinal d'Amboise employed by Louis XII of France, knowing of the English king's liking for precious relics, presented him with the thigh bone of St. George enclosed in silver. On St. George's day, 23 April, Henry went in solemn procession to St. Paul's where the saintly relic was displayed before a pious multitude of people.

Bacon's contention that the statutes made during Henry's reign were his pre-eminent virtue cannot be sustained. He thought that the king may justly be celebrated for the best laws since the time of Edward I.

Henry's health was extremely poor by the spring of 1509. He suffered from consumption and according to one eminent authority, J. Gardner, from pains in the chest and difficulty of respiration. By late March, he was known to be dying, though we are not aware of the exact symptoms. He lay in bed in his palace of Richmond 'abiding the sharp assaults of death'. It was no sudden death. According to a Swiss historian, who published a book in Basle in 1610, Henry ordered that his blood should be sprinkled on the walls of the room in which he died, but there is little confirmation from other sources. It was a Saturday 21 April, according to Kingsford Chronicles. 'This yere uppon the Saturday next before St. Georges Day died the King our soueraigne at his lodging called Richemount.' He was aged fifty-two.

He had given his executors precise instructions as to his funeral, providing that a monument should be erected so that he could lie beside his cherished Queen Elizabeth of York, who had died six years earlier. Acting on his last wishes, his executors, including his beloved mother, who survived him only a few months, invited the Florentine sculptor Pietro Torrigiano, to come to England to create the most beautiful Renaissance monuments in England. Henry and Elizabeth lie side by side in their tomb with cherubs seated at each corner. Above the tombs is the red dragon of Wales, Henry's personal symbol when he planned to invade England in 1485. In Bacon's immortal phrase 'he dwelleth more richly dead, in the monument of his tomb, than he did alive in Richmond, or any of his palaces'. It was characteristic of Henry, when providing for 10,000 masses to be said for his soul, to mention the sum to be paid for each mass and to insert how many masses should be said to honour various celestial powers. The Henry VII Chapel was not completed until 1519.

It was Bishop Fisher of Rochester who preached Henry's funeral sermon on 10 May in St. Paul's, a worthy tribute. His mother, the countess of Richmond and Derby, made the special request to her intimate friend to have it printed. Fisher praises the king for:

> his politic wisdom ('polytyque wysedome') in gouernance, his wytee alway quyche (quick) and redy, his reason pyththy and substancyall, his memory fresshe (fresh) and holdynge his notable experience, fortunate counsels and wyse delyberacyon, his speche grecyous in dyverse languages.

Bishop Fisher said Henry's mighty power was:

> dredd ever where ... his profperitie in batayle ayenft his enemies was meruaylous, his delynge in tyne perylles and dangers was cold, and sobre with grete hardynesse.

There is in Fisher's *cri de coeur* a bitter lament.

A Kynge Henry Kynge Henry yf thou were alyve agayne, marry one that is here present now wolde pretende a full grete pityte and tendernesse upon the.

He must surely mean that the tone of many people critical of the king today when he could no longer defend himself against their remonstrances would be very different if he was still alive.

A few months later, the bishop was to pay a further noble tribute to the Lady Margaret, Henry VIII's mother, not omitting to mention her curious fears in times of prosperity or adversity to follow: 'For whom the king her sone was crowned in all that grete trymphe and glorye, she wepte meruayllously'. 'And lyke wyfe at the grete tryumphe of the maryage of Prince Arthur.'

It was surely providential that England so bitterly divided by ruinous war should be united by a wise king, who possessing little hereditary right to his throne, nevertheless ruled over her with surprising efficiency. One priceless gift Henry VII bequeaths his son was an undisputed succession.

APPENDIX ITALIANS TOOK A GREAT INTEREST IN JOHN CABOT'S VOYAGES

(See Calendar of State Papers, Milan Vol. I, No. 553, Milan Archives (Potenze Estere: Inghiltena))

(Raimondo de Raimondi de Sancino writing to the Duke of Milan, 18 December 1497)

Perhaps amid the numerous occupations of Your Excellency, it may not weary you to hear how His Majesty (Henry VII) here has gained a part of Asia, without a stroke of the sword. There is in this kingdom a man of the people, Messer Zoane Caboto by name, of kindly wit and a most expert mariner. Having observed that the sovereigns first of Portugal and then of Spain had occupied unknown islands, he decided to make a similar acquisition for His Majesty ... he committed himself to fortune in a little ship with eighteen persons. He started from Bristol, a port on the west of this kingdom ... past Ireland ... and then bore towards the north in order to sail to the east ... After having wandered for some time he at length arrived at the mainland, where he hoisted the royal standard, and took possession for the King here ...

This Messer Zoane, as a foreigner and a poor man, would not have obtained credence, had it not been that his companions, who are practically all English and from Bristol, testified that he spoke the truth ... What is much more, His Majesty who is wise and not prodigal, also gives him some credence, because he is giving him a fairly good provision, since his return, so Messer Zoane himself tells me ...

(I have made use of Peter Firstbrook's translation of the original Italian of this letter.)

NOTES

Chapter I

1. The unpublished thesis of Roger Thomas. Swansea University Library.
2. *Chronicle of London* edited by Tyrrell and Nicolas (1827), 123.
3. *Henry VI*, B. Wolffe (1981). English Monarchs series.
4. *Lancaster & York : The Wars of the Roses*, Alison Weir (First published 1995).
5. Chronicle attributed to William Gregory, Mayor of London 1452/2. *The historical collections of a citizen of London in the fifteenth century.* Camden Society New Series XVII (1876).
6. See *The Herberts of Raglan* unpublished MA Thesis (1968) by D.H. Thomas, Cardiff University Library.
7. *The Wars of the Roses*, Desmond Seward (1995), p. 131.
8. *The King's Mother,* Jones and Underwood, (1991).
9. Ibid.
10. See Jasper Tudor. The Lancashire Champion. *The Making of the Tudor Dynasty*, Ralph A. Griffiths & Roger S. Thomas (1985).

Chapter II

1. *Henry VI*, Part Three, Act III, Scene VI.
2. *The Welsh Historical Review.* A History of the Transactions of the Anglesey Antiquarian Society for 1961.
3. *A History of the Island of Mona*, Angharad Lloyd.
4. Bibliothèque Nationale, Paris, 6982 fol. 326.
5. See *Edward IV*, Charles Ross (edition published 1997).
6. *Usurpation of Richard III*, edited and translated C.A.J. Armstrong, p. 67.

Chapter III

1. *The Historie of King Richarde, the Thirde*, Thomas More, page 6 (1883 edition).
2. Ibid. This scene is taken from More's vivid account.

3. Original preserved at the *Bibliothè que Municipale* at Lille. It has been translated from the Latin by Armstrong.

4. He lived from 1443-1508.

5. *Richard III : England's Black Legend*, Desmond Seward (1983).

6. *History of England* (1883) edited by J. Rawson Lumby.

7. Ibid. More's *History of England*.

8. *Lancaster and York : The War of the Roses*, Alison Weir,

9. See his *Richard III*, edited A.N. Kincois, pages 63, 64.

10. Add. MSS 9.398 British Library. Henry acknowledges the loan.

11. Pages 328 and 329. Appendix 6. *Henry VII*, Professor S.B. Chrimes.

12. Ibid. *The Wars of the Roses*, Desmond Seward.

13. *A History of France From the Death of Louis XI,* John C. Bridge, Vol. I 1483-93.

14. Ibid.

15. Polydore Vergil, *op. cit.* 201-204.

16. Riley, *Crowland Chronicle.*

17. *Elizabeth of York : Tudor Queen.* Nancy Lenz Harvey.

18. I. Heywood: Most pleasant song of the Lady Bessy.

19. Ibid. *Henry VII*, S.B. Chrimes, page 30.

Chapter IV

1. *The Princes in the Tower* (1978), Elizabeth Jenkins, page. 204.

2. *Continuation of the History of Croyland.*

3. Ibid., page 499.

4. Ibid., page 499.

5. One of Richard's chief friends.

6. *Letters of the Kings of England* (1846). James Orchard, Hallingwell Phillips.

7. Ibid.

8. *Continuation of the History of England.*

9. *Wars of the Roses.* Desmond Seward, p.. 304.

10. The Herberts of Raglan, M.A. unpublished thesis.

11. *Henry VII,* S.B. Chrimes, p. 44.

12. Quoted from Sir John Wynne *A Book of Wales.*

13. *The Battle of Bosworth Field,* D.T. Williams (1973).

14. Three Books of Polydore Vergil, edited by Sir Henry Ellis.

15. Father of Charles Brandon, a close friend of Henry VIII. He later created him Duke of Suffolk.

16. My accounts of Bosworth are based on J. Gairdner's *Archaeologia* or *Miscellaneous Tracts relating to Antiquity* and many contemporary and later accounts.

Chapter V

1. *The Transformation of Medieval England*, John A.F. Thomson (1983), 1370-1529.
2. *Continuation of the History of Croyland*, page 512.
3. *Henry VII*, S.B. Chrimes, page 66.
4. *Plumpton Correspondence* (Camden Society 1835).
5. Page 62.
6. *Materials for the History of the Reign of Henry VII from Original Documents in the Public Record Office*, edited by Rev. William Campbell.
7. Gladys Temperley, *Henry VII*.
8. See *A Relation or Rather a True Account of the Island of England*. Translated from the Italian with notes, Charlotte Auguste Sneyd.
9. *Materials For The History Of The Reign Of Henry VII From Original Documents In The Public Record Office* edited by Rev. William Campbell.
10. A late sixteenth century MS. Egerton 985, fols. 416-48 now in British Library gives an account of Henry's coronation.
11. See article by Peter Holmes. The Great Council in the Reign of Henry VII. *English Historical Review*.
12. *A Relation or Rather a True Account of the Island of England*. Translated from the Italian with notes by Sneyd.
13. *Elizabeth of York : Tudor Queen*, Nancy Lenz Harvey.
14. *The Rebellion of Humphrey Stafford*. C.H. Williams, *English Historical Review*. Edited by C.W. Previte Orton.
15. Ibid. Bacon, *Henry VII*, 211.
16. *Elizabeth of York : Tudor Queen*, Nancy Lenz Harvey.
17. *Margaret of York*. Duchess of Burgundy, Christine Weighman (first published in England, 1989).
18. Ibid., page 159.
19. *Earlier Tudors*, 1485-1555. Mackie.
20. *Henry VII*, S.B. Chrimes.
21. Select Papers Chiefly Relating to English Antiquities. Published from the original in the possession of John Ives.

Chapter VI

1. *The Earlier Tudors*, 1485-1558, Mackie.
2. Ibid.
3. She was the daughter and heiress of Charles the Bold, Duke of Burgundy, by his second wife Isabella of Bourbon.
4. Stowe's *Annals*.

5.   *A Relation or Rather a True Account of the Island of England.* Note 51. (Camden Society).

6.   See C.S. Goldingham's 'The Navy under Henry VII and accounts and inventories of Henry VII', edited by M. Oppenheim, Navy Records Office (1896).

7.   Ibid.

8.   *Henry VII*, S.B. Chrimes.

9.   *A Relation or Rather a True Account of the Island of England*, note 61, page 103.

10.   Bacon, *Henry VII*, ed. Lumby 192, 3.

11.   *The Transformation of Medieval England*, pages 121 and 122.

12.   Ibid., page 123.

Chapter VII

1.   *Jewish Hostorical Society Transactions.* Vol. 9. 1918-20.

2.   The Story of Perkin Warbeck taken from the *History of the Life and Reign of Richard III* by James Gairdner, page 264.

3.   See *Margaret of York*, Duchess of Burgundy, 1446-1503, Weightman (1989).

4.   Ibid., page 170.

5.   *Calendar of State Papers*, Spanish.

6.   See article in *The English Historical Review.* 14 Jan.-October 1899.

7.   A sixteenth century copy of his trial was found in Camb. MS. Ex 3.4 and published by W.A.J. Archbold, E.H.R., XIV (July 1899). See S.B. Chrimes *Henry VII*, page 85. 529-34.

8.   *Calendar of State Papers*, Spanish. Studied in the Public Record Office, Kew.

9.   *Earlier Tudors.* 1485-1558. Mackie.

10.   *English Historical Review.* Mark Stoyle's article, May 1997.

11.   Page 105.

12.   *Earlier Tudors.* 1485-1558. Mackie.

13.   Letters written in French. See Gairdner *Richard III*. The story of Perkin Warbeck from original documents, page 329.

14.   *Henry VIII*, S.B. Chrimes.

15.   *Italian Renaissance Studies* edited by E.J. Jacob (1960).

16.   Ibid.

Chapter VIII

1.   *Earlier Tudors.* 1485-1555. Mackie, Page 225.

2.   See *The Voyages of John and Sebastian Cabot.* (Published for the Historical Association, 1937).

3.   J.A. Williamson.
4.   *The Voyages of John and Sebastian Cabot.*
5.   *The Great Seamen of Elizabeth I.* Bryan Bevan, page 24.

Chapter IX

1   *Henry VII's relations with Scotland and Ireland* 1485-98. Agnes Conway with a chapter on the Acts of the Poynings Parliament 1494-5 by Edmund Curtis.
2.   Ibid.

Chapter X

1.   See *Catherine of Aragon*, Garret Mattingly's masterly biography. Paperback 1942.
2.   *Calendar of State Papers, Spanish.* I.132, 136, 139.
3.   *Miscellaneous Pieces De Rebus Britann.* Collecteana and Sequendo, Vol. V, page 353.
4.   Mattingly. *Op. cit.*
5.   *De Rebus Britann., op. cit.*, Vol. V.
6.   *Calendar of State Papers, Spanish.* Public Record Office, Kew.
7.   *Henry VII*, S.B. Chrimes.
8.   Vol. V, page 356.
9.   *De Rebus Britann., op. cit.*, Vol. V, page. 361.
10. This important incident is beautifully related by Leland in his *Collecteana*, Vol. V, pages 373-4.

Chapter XI

1.   *Henry VII's Relations with Scotland and Ireland* 1485-98.
2.   *The Sisters of Henry VIII*, Hester Chapman (1969).
3.   *Princesses of England*, Vol. IV (1854).
4.   *Original letters illustrative of English History with notes*, Henry Ellis, Vol. I, Letter XX.
5.   Ibid.
6.   William Dunbar, Scotland's poet, wrote this poem and others praising Queen Margaret.
7.   *The Earls of Derby* 1485-1985. See chapter on the Lord Stanley by J.J. Bagley.
8.   *The Mad Queen of Spain*, Michael Prawdin (1935). Translated by Edwena Cedor.
9.   *Henry VII*, S.B. Chrimes.

10. For accounts of Philip's visit to Windsor, see Bergenroth *Calendar of State Papers, Spanish* No. 451, Brown, Venetian Calendar 862-869.
11. *Calendar of State Papers, Spanish* 1498-1530. Public Record Office, Kew.
12. De Puebla to King Ferdinand. 7 Sept. 1507.

Chapter XII

1. *The Princes in the Tower*, Elizabeth Jenkins, page 193.
2. *The Life of Sir Thomas More*, Peter Ackroyd (1998).
3. Landsdowne, MSS, 127 f. 34, British Library. Edmund Dudley's account book, also Mackie's *Earlier Tudors*.
4. *Henry VII*, S.B. Chrimes.
5. *Humanism in England during the Fifteenth Century*, Weiss.

Chapter XIII

1. *England under the Tudors*, Wilhelm Busch, translated from the German by A.M. Todd, London, 1895.
2. Ibid. *England under the Tudors*, Busch.
3. See *The Tudors*. Christopher Morris. Fontana-Collins (1976).
4. *Henry VII*, S.B. Chrimes.
5. *Op. cit., England under the Tudors*, Busch.
6. H. Ellis, *Original Letters*, 1st. Series I, 1825.46.
7. *Henry VII*, S.B. Chrimes, page 235.
8. *Catherine of Aragon*, Garrett Mattingley.
9. *Calendar of State Papers, Spanish*.
10. *Letters and Papers of Henry VII*. Vol. I, Part 2, page 512.
11. *Calendar of State Papers, Spanish*. Public Record Office, Kew.
12. *Henry VII*, Gladys Temperley (1914).
13. *The Life of Sir Thomas More*, Peter Ackroyd (1998).
14. Dr. Roy Strong, *Tudor and Jacobean Portraits*, 2 Vols. (1969).

Chapter XIV

1. Author of *England under the Tudors*. See G.R. Elton, *Henry VII: Rapacity and Remorse* (1974).
2. Transactions of the Royal Historical Society Fourth Series, Vol. XV (1932) has her prize essay Edmund Dudley, Minister of Henry VII.
3. See edition edited with notes by Rev. J. Lawson Lumby (1881), page 217.
4. Page 216.

5. Edited with an introduction by D.M. Brodie, Cambridge University Press, 1945.
6. *Henry VII*, S.B. Chrimes.
7. Published in E.H.R. LXXXVII, 1972, 82-99.
8. *The Will of Henry VII*, ed. T. Astle (1775).
9. *Henry VII*, S.B. Chrimes.
10. E.101 MSS. Bundle 415.28.
11. *Henry VII*, Gladys Temperley.
12. *Letters and papers of Henry VII*, II.379.

BIBLIOGRAPHY

Bacon, Francis, *History of the Reign of Henry VII* with notes by the Rev. J. Lawson Lumby (1881).

Bagley, J.J., *The Earls of Derby 1485-1985.* see chapter on Lord Stanley .

Bennett, Michael, *The Battle of Bosworth 1485.*

Bevan, Bryan, *The Great Seamen of Elizabeth I*, page 24 (1971).

Bridge, John C., *A History of France from the death of Louis XI*, vol. I (1921).

British Library Add. MSS 7099.

   –Harleian MSS 225.

Busch, Wilhelm, *England under the Tudors.* Translation from the German by A.M. Todd. London (1895).

Calendar of State Papers, Spanish, 1498-1531, ed. Bergenroth. Public Record Office.

Calendar of State Papers, Venetian, No. 451, 862-69.

Calendar of State Papers, Milanese, particularly page 323.

Chapman, Hester, *The Sisters of Henry VIII* (Margaret Tudor and Mary Tudor) (1969).

Chrimes, S.B., *Henry VII.* A scholarly work with a very detailed bibliography.

Chronicles of London, ed. C.L. Kingsford.

Conway, Agnes, *Henry VII's Relations with Scotland and Ireland,* 1485-1498 (1932).

Dudley, Edmund, *The Tree of the Commonwealth* (1509), ed. D.M. Brodie.

Ellis, Henry, *Original Letters illustrative of English history. 1st Series,* vol. I, 1825-46.

Everett-Green, *Princesses of England* (1854), vol. IV .

Firstbrook, Peter, *The voyage of the Matthew. John Cabot and the discovery of North America.* Foreword by H.R.H. the Duke of Edinburgh (1997).

Fisher, John, *The English Works of John Fisher Bishop of Rochester.* First collected by John E.B. Mayor. Part I, MDCCCLXXVI (1876).

Foss, Peter J., *The Battle of Bosworth, Aug. 22, 1485.*

Gairdner, J., *Archaeologia : Miscellaneous Tracts relating to Antiquity.* Published by the Society of Antiquaries of London.

Gairdner, J. (ed.), *Chronicle attributed to William Gregory Mayor of London 1451/2. The Historical Collection of a Citizen of London in Fifteenth Century.* (Camden Society New Series XVIV, 1876).

Gairdner, J. (ed.), *Letters and Papers illustrative of the reign of Henry VII.*

Gairdner, J. (ed.), *Memorials of Henry VII*, (Rolls Series, 1858), vols. I and II.

Gairdner, J., *Richard III*. The story of Perkin Warbeck from original documents, page 329.

Gairdner, J., *Archaeologia : Miscellaneous Tracts relating to Antiquity*. Published by the Society of Antiquaries of London.

Goldingham, C.S., *The Navy under Henry VII* and *Accounts and inventories of Henry VII*, ed. M. Oppenheim. Navy Records Office (1896).

Guy, John, *Tudor England*, (1990).

Haigh, Peter, *The Military Campaign of the Wars of the Roses*.

Halliwell-Phillips, J.O., *Letters of the Kings of England* (1846).

Halstead, Caroline A., *Life of Margaret Beaufort* (1839).

Henry VII's will printed for the Editor and sold by T.Payne at the Mews-Gate at Horace's Head, Fleet Street (1775)

History of the Transactions of the Anglesey Society (1961).

Holmes, Peter, 'The Great Council in the Reign of Henry VII'. *English Historical Review*.

Jacob, E.J., *Italian Renaissance Studies*.

James and Underwood, *The King's Mother* (Lady Margaret Beaufort), 1991.

Jenkins, Elizabeth, *The Princes in the Tower* (1978).

Leland, John, *Miscellaneous Pieces de Rebus Britann. Collecteana*, vol. 5, page 353 et seq.

Lenz Harvey, Nancy, *Elizabeth of York : Tudor Queen* (1973).

Macdougall, Norman, *James IV : The Stewart Dynasty in Scotland* (1997).

Mackie, J.D., *The Earlier Tudors*, 1485-1558 (1952).

Mancini, Dominic, *De Occupatione Regni anglie per Ricardum Tercium*. (Translated from the Latin by Armstrong). A contemporary work.

Manuscripts - Henry VII's Household accounts

E 101/414/16. Heron's book of payments. 15 to 16 Henry VII.

E 101/414/6.   Heron's book of payments. 11 to 13 Henry VII.

E 101/415/3. Heron's book of payments.. 15 to 18 Henry VII.

E 36/210. Queen Elizabeth of York's book of household accounts. (There is only one account book for the Queen.)

Markham, Clements, *Richard III*.

Mattingly, Garrett, *Catherine of Aragon* (1942).

Mattingly, Garrett, 'The Reputation of Dr. Puebla', *English Historical Review* LV (1940).

More, Thomas, *The Historie of King Richarde The Thirde* (1883 edition).

Morris, Christopher, *The Tudors* (1955). Chapter on Henry VII.

Pollard, A.F. (ed.), *The reign of Henry VII from contemporary sources*. –*Richard III and the Princes in the Tower* (1957).

Prawdin, Michael, *The Mad Queen of Spain*. Translated by Edwena Cedor (1935).

Riland's *Croyland Chronicle. Continuation of the History of Croyland*.

Ross, Charles, *Edward IV* (Yale University Edition), 1974.

Roth, Cecil, *Perkin Warbeck. His Jewish master.* Jewish Historical Society Transactions, vol. 9, 1918-20.

Rouse, A.L., *Bosworth Field* (1966).

Routh, E.M.G, *Lady Margaret Beaufort* (1924).

Select Papers Chiefly Relating to English Antiquities. Published from the original in the possession of John Ives.

Seward, Desmond, *Richard III : England's Black Legend* (1983).
  – The Wars of the Roses (1995).

Shakespeare, William, *Henry VI*, Part III.

Sneyd, C.A. (ed.), *A Relation of the Island of England* (Camden Society, 1847).

Stanley, William, Article in the *English Historical Review.* Jan.-Oct. 1899.

Stoyle, Mark, article in *English Historical Review* (May 1997).

Strong, Roy, *Tudor and Jacobean Portraits.*

Temperley, Gladys, *Henry VII* (1914).

Thomas, D.H., 'The Political Career, Estates and Connection of Jasper Tudor, Earl of Pembroke, Duke of Bedford died 1494'. Unpublished Ph.D. thesis, University of Wales, Swansea, 1971.
  –'The Herberts of Raglan as supporters of the House of York in the second half of the fifteenth century'. Unpublished M.A. thesis, University of Wales, Cardiff, 1968.

Thompson, John A.F., *The Transformation of Medieval England* 1370-1529. (1983).

Turell and Nicholas (ed), *Chronicle of London* (1827).

Vergil, Polydore, contemporary Italian historian.

Weighman, Christine, *Margaret of York : Duchess of Burgundy* 1446-1503 (1989).

Welsh Historical Review.

Williams, D, 'The Welsh Tudors'. Article in *History Today*, Vol, IV, 1954.

Williams, Neville, *The Life and Times of Henry VII* (1973).

Williamson, J.A., *The Cabot Voyages and Bristol Discovery under Henry VII.* Hakluyt Society (1962).

Wynne, John, *A Book of Wales* (1553-1626).

Williams, C.H., 'The Rebellion of Humphrey Stafford'. *English Historical Review.*

INDEX

duke of *see* Francis II
Henry Tudor's exile 13-15, 22-7, 38, 41, 44, 46, 53, 64, 73, 106
independence 25
treaty with 53
Brodie, Miss D.M. 107
Broughton, Sir Thomas 51, 85
Bruges 61
Buck, Sir George 31
Buckingham, Harry *see* Stafford, Henry
Buckingham Rebellion 21-2, 24, 27, 34, 73, 93
Burgavenny, Lord George Neville 58
Burgundy 62
Butler, Lady Eleanor 19
Butlers, earls of Ormond 73

Cabot, John 70-2
Cabot, Ludovico 70
Cabot, Sancio 70
Cabot, Sebastian 70, 72
Cabra, count of 77-8
Cade, Jack 64
Cadwalleder (last King of the Britons) 2
Caerleon, Dr Lewis 21-2
Calais 69, 87, 107
Cambray, bishop of 67
Canterbury Cathedral 93
Capell, Sir William 107
Capello, Francesco 45
Carmarthen 34
Carmarthen Castle, Wales 4
Castile 87
    succession to 86
    see also Isabella of Castile; Joanna of Castile
Castle of Bois-de-Vincennes 1
Castle Hedingham, Essex 57
Castle of Koeur-la-Petite, duchy of Bar 21

Catesby, William 30-1, 39
Cathay 71-2
Catherine of Berain (granddaughter of Sir Rowland de Vielleville) 14
Catherine, Princess of Aragon 76-7
    dowry 77, 81, 101, 103
    Dr. Rodrigo de Puebla 78, 81, 100, 103
    father Ferdinand 82, 89, 100, 102-3
    Fuensalida 103
    Henry VII 78, 82, 89, 100, 102-3
    possible marriages
        Henry (VIII) 81-2
        Prince Henry 81-2, 89, 100, 103-4, 113
    Prince Arthur, marriage to 54, 58, 61, 67, 75-82
    Princess of Wales 76
    return to Spain 81
    widowhood 82, 89, 102-3
    Windsor Castle 88
Caxton, William 61, 99
    The Book of Faylles of Armes and of Chivalrie 99
Cerdagne and Roussillon provinces 54
Charles of Gwent *see* Maximilian, Archduke Charles
Charles VI, King of France 1
Charles VIII, King of France 19, 25, 32, 53-4
    marriage to daughter of Duke Francis of Brittany) 60
    Perkin Warbeck 60, 64, 67
Charterhouse at Sheen 66
Chaucer, Geoffrey 4
Cheapside, stocks 67
Cheney, Sir John 38
Chepstow 12
Cheyney, John 24
Chrimes, S.B. 12

Essex, earl of 44
Exeter 65-6, 77

Fabyan, Robert 92-3
Fenny Drayton 36
Ferandez, Fray Diego 102-3
Ferdinand of Aragon
    adulterous relationships 46
    Archduke Philip Maximilian (son in-law) 88
    Catherine, Princess of Aragon 82, 89, 100, 102-3
    de Fuensalida 100-1
    Dr. de Puebla 100
    Henry VII 39, 87-9, 100
    and Isabella of Castile 85
        daughters
            Catherine *see* Catherine, Princess of Aragon
            Isabella 77-8, 85
        Joanna of Castile 86, 88-9
        Jewish servants 76
        marriage 54, 65, 85
        Perkin Warbeck 61, 67
        relations with Henry VII 81, 85
    League of Cambrai (1508) 112
    remarriage to Germaine de Foix 88
    Sebastian Cabot 71-2
    succession to Castile 86
Fernandez, Francisco 71
Fernandez, Joao? 71
Ferrara, duke of 95
Ferrers, Sir Thomas 34
Fisher, Dr. John
    bishop of Rochester 4-5, 93, 99-100
    Henry VII's funeral sermon 114-5
    Lady Margaret (mother of Henry VII) 115

Fitzgerald, Gerald, eighth Earl of Kildare 49, 74
Fitzgerald, Thomas 51
Fitzwalter, Lord 7
Flamank, Thomas 64-5
Flanders 22, 24, 26-7, 55, 62
Flemish and Italian artists 95
Florence, treaty with 55
Forest, Miles 92
Fortescue, Sir John 31, 34
Fossedyke, Lambert, Abbot of Croyland Monastery 33
Fox Channel 71-2
Fox, Richard, bishop of Exeter, of Bath and Wells, of Durham and of Winchester 24, 63, 65-6, 93, 101, 103, 108, 112
France
    Council of Regency, relations with England 27
    Henry Tudor 30-2, 34, 53
    peace with England 53, 62
    policy of acquiring Brittany 27
    and Scotland, league between 84
    ship 56
    war with England (1492) 53, 112
Francis II, Duke of Brittany 13-15, 23, 25-7, 53
Franco-Breton war 54
Frion (Former French Secretary of Henry VII) 60
Froissart, Jean 99
Furness, Lancashire, rebel army 50
Fychan, Ednyfed 1

Gairdner (author of biography of King Richard) 21
Gardiner, Stephen, bishop of Winchester 43
Gardner, J. 113

George of Clarence (brother of Edward IV), earl of Richmond 9, 12, 17

George duke of Clarence (brother of Edward IV), earl of Richmond
born in Dublin (1449) 49
declared a bastard 18, 26, 29
married to Isabel Neville 11-12
Queen Elizabeth Woodville 16

German mercenaries 51

Gigli, Giovanni (later bishop of Worcester) 68, 94

Gigli, Silvestro (later bishop of Worcester) 94

Glastonbury 66

Glendower, Owen 1

Gloucester, Humphrey duke of (younger brother of Henry V) 2-4

Gonsalvey, João 71

Gordon, Lady Catherine (daughter of second earl of Huntly)
marriages
Christopher Ashton 66
James Strangeway 66
Matthew Cradock 66
Perkin Warbeck 63, 65-6

Graffudd, Elis 1

Grafton 31

Granadan wars 77

Gravesend 22

Great Councils 45, 49, 64

Great Malvern Priory Church, Magnificat window 105

Green, John 92

Greenwich Palace 46, 48, 51, 69, 81, 96, 99, 101

Grey, Dame Elizabeth *see* Woodville, Queen Elizabeth

Grey, Thomas, marquess of Dorset (son of Queen Elizabeth Woodville) 23-4, 28, 33

Greyfriars, Carmarthen 4

Griffith of Penrhyn, Sir William 14

Guildford 44
Lady 78

Hall, Edward 2, 36-7, 50, 60

Hames Castle near Calais 31

Hapsburgs
in Spain 87
see also Maximilian, Emperor

Harfleur sailing 34

Harlech Castle, Wales 11

Haseley, Edward (later Dean Warwick) 10

Hastings, Lord William 7, 17-19, 34, 39

Hatfield, bishop of Ely's palace 2

Henry IV, King, Eltham Palace 96

Henry, Prince, duke of York (Henry VII's younger son) 48, 55, 64, 68, 77, 79-81, 90-1, 110
birth at Greenwich Palace 96
Catherine of Aragon 81-2, 89, 100-1, 103-4, 113
preparation for kingship 90-1
suitors 89

Henry V, King 1

Henry VI, King (son of Henry V born 1421) 1, 3-5, 8-9
Battle of Towton 21
buried in St. George's Chapel, Windsor 97
Council 2
death in Tower (1471) 14, 17
favours to Owen Tudor and half-brothers Edmund and Jasper 3
Henry Tudor 12
love of rare animals 98
mother's marriage to Owen Tudor 3
Percy family 36

144

Waterford 73
Weir, Alison 12
Welles, John (later to marry Cecily of York) 24
Wells 64
West Country, Perkin Warbeck 65
West, Dr. Nicholas, earl of Surrey 84, 101
Westminster, parliament 42
Westminster Abbey 2, 7, 97
  Lady Chapel 3, 96
  chapel of Henry VII 82, 96-7, 114
  coronations
    Henry VII 44
    Richard III 20
  Queen Elizabeth Woodville 20-1, 28-9
  Queen of Scot's Chapel 6
  St. Paul's Chapel 94
  shrine of St Edward 69
Westminster Hall 52, 67, 79-80
  Sir William Stanley tried for treason (1495) 62
Westminster, Palace of 66-7, 72
  apartments 29
  Henry III's painted chamber 96
  Henry VII 96
White, John (son of Thomas) 12-13
White Moors 36
White, Thomas 12-13
White Tower 17
Whitesand Bay near Land's End 65
Wilford, Ralph 69
Williamson, J.A. 70
Willoughby de Broke, Lord 77
Willoughby, Sir Robert 24, 40
Wiltshire, earl of 7
Wimborne, burial place of duke and duchess of Somerset 99
Winchester 47

Windsor Castle
  birth of Henry VI 1
  Catherine of Aragon 88
  Henry VII 87, 104
  St. George's Chapel 43, 96-7, 104
Witherly 36
Woebley, Hertfordshire 12
Woking Old Hall 8-9
Wolffe, Dr. Bertram 3
Wolsey, Cardinal Thomas 93
Woodstock in Oxfordshire 96
Woodstock, Thomas of 20
Woodville, Catherine, son Edward Stafford 43
Woodville, Catherine, marriages
  Henry Stafford 20
  Jasper Tudor 42
Woodville, Edward, Lord Scales 23-4, 27, 53
Woodville, Lionel, bishop of Salisbury 23
Woodville, Queen Elizabeth (wife of Edward IV) 11, 15, 18, 20-2, 28
  Bermondsey convent 49
  daughter Elizabeth 16, 19, 21, 28
  forfeited lands to the queen 51
  Henry VII 47-9
  Richard III 28-9
  Westminster Abbey 20-1, 28-9
Woodville, Sir Richard 32
Worcester 47
  Cathedral, funeral of Prince Arthur 80
Wynn of Gwydir, Sir John 2

York 36, 47, 83
York, Anne (daughter of Edward IV) 28

York, Bridget (daughter of Edward IV) 28

York, Cecily duchess of (daughter of Edward IV) 16, 18, 22, 26, 28, 48
marriage to John Welles 24
second marriage to Thomas Kymber 99

York, duke of (second son of Henry VII) created 1494 14

York, Edward of (later Edward IV) 7

York, Katherine (daughter of Edward IV) 28

York and Lancaster, unity of Houses of 15, 50

York, Princess Elizabeth of (daughter of Edward IV) 16, 19, 21-2, 24-5, 29-31, 40
marriage to Henry VII 42
see also Elizabeth of York, Queen

York, Richard duke of (son of Edward IV) 15-19, 21, 49, 60-1, 80
imposter 60, 63, 66
sons *see* Edward IV, George duke of Clarence; Richard III

Yorkists 3, 5, 7-8, 25, 60
Anglo-Irish supporters 73
dynasty 61
exiles 61
heir to the throne of England 40, 67
insurrection 49
king Edward IV 15
plot (1486) 48
Pretender *see* Warbeck, Perkin
victory at Barnet (1471) 12

Yorkshire, taxation 56